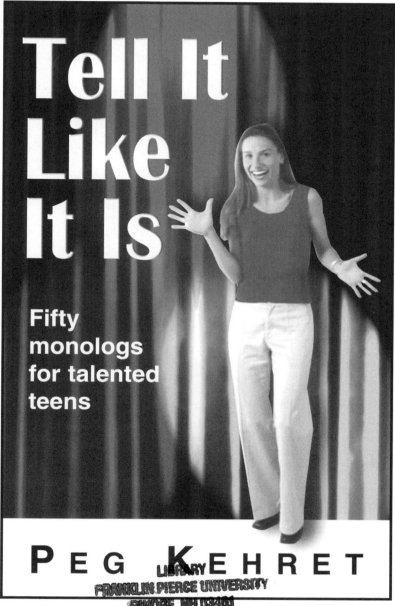

Tell It Like It Is

Fifty
monologs
for talented
teens

PEG KEHRET

MERIWETHER PUBLISHING LTD.
Colorado Springs, Colorado

Meriwether Publishing Ltd., Publisher
PO Box 7710
Colorado Springs, CO 80933-7710

Associate editor: Arthur L. Zapel
Assistant editor: Audrey Scheck
Cover design: Jan Melvin

Library of Congress Cataloging-in-Publication Data

Kehret, Peg.
  Tell it like it is : fifty monologs for talented teens / by Peg Kehret.
    p. cm.
  ISBN-13: 978-1-56608-144-3 (pbk.)
  ISBN-10: 1-56608-144-0
1. Monologues--Juvenile literature. 2. Acting--Juvenile Literature.
3. Teenagers--Drama. I. Title.
PN2080.K35 2007
808.82'45--dc22

                                        2007000083

            1   2   3   07   08   09

For Marilyn Kamcheff,
who walked beside me in the darkness,
helping me laugh through my tears,

and, always, in memory of Carl.

Table of Contents

Acknowledgments

Three books were especially useful in historical research:

Dust to Eat: Drought and Depression in the 1930s by Michael L. Cooper (copyright 2004: Clarion Books, New York); *The Power of One: Daisy Bates and the Little Rock Nine* by Judith Bloom Fradin and Dennis Brindell Fradin (copyright 2004: Clarion Books, New York); and *The Old West: The Women* by Joan Swallow Rieiter (copyright 1978: Time-Life Books, Alexandria, Virginia). Susan Michaels of Pasado's Safe Haven (http://www.pasadosafehaven.org) told me about Katie's second chance ("A Home for Katie," page 84). "Roadside Rescue" (page 36) is based on an article published in *The News Tribune* (Tacoma, Washington).

Special thanks to Art Zapel, who edited my first book and who asked me to write this one, and to my family who, intentionally or not, provided the material for many of these monologs.

1. Too Much Homework

1   My teachers have an ongoing competition to see who can pile on
2   the most homework every week. Mrs. Wetherby is winning. She
3   thinks every student in her class exists solely to learn more about
4   American history.

5   My parents created an unfortunate rule that homework must be
6   finished before any other activities on school nights. No exceptions. If
7   my house catches fire, I'd better finish my math problems before I dial
8   nine-one-one.

9   Because of this silly rule, I do no other activities on school nights.
10   The only person who could finish all of my homework and still have
11   time for anything else would have to be a clone of Einstein.

12   Do I feel like baking cookies? Too bad. History homework is more
13   important than culinary skills. Do I want to instant message my
14   friends? Forget it; there's math to do first. As for watching TV or
15   renting a movie, ha! By the time I finish my homework, it's too late to
16   start a movie, and the only shows on TV are ancient reruns.

17   It isn't that I'm a poor student. I'm not the genius of the century,
18   but I have a decent grade point average, and I've never flunked
19   anything. That isn't good enough for Mrs. Wetherby.

20   Her idea of a fab birthday party would be to have everyone come
21   dressed in Revolutionary War costumes and take turns reciting the
22   Declaration of Independence.

23   Why don't we have classes in subjects that matter? I would not
24   mind doing homework about Seven Ways to Get Rid of Zits or Why
25   Chocolate is More Nutritious than Cauliflower. I'd even be willing to
26   study English Literature if I could read *People* magazine instead of
27   books by writers who died before I was even born. Have you noticed
28   that famous authors are usually dead? Especially poets. The poets I
29   have to study probably died of broken hearts because nobody liked

1 what they wrote.

2   Mrs. Wetherby says it's important to study history because history
3 tends to repeat itself. I'll tell you what repeats itself and that is Mrs.
4 Wetherby. She is especially fond of reminding us, over and over, that,
5 "A stitch in time saves nine."

6   You'd think we were taking a sewing class. To her, a stitch in time
7 means studying for the Friday quiz each week. Proper preparation will
8 prevent disaster on the test questions. Oh, sure, I know that if I study
9 for the quiz, I'll get more correct answers than if I don't study. So why
10 can't she just tell us to study instead of quoting a proverb that's been
11 around longer than Santa Claus?

12   "A stitch in time saves nine" can also be interpreted to mean,
13 "Don't wait until the night before your term paper is due to begin
14 researching it."

15   Mrs. Wetherby says she quotes proverbs because she wants us to
16 remember what she says, and it's easier to remember something that
17 rhymes. Well, I hate to tell her this, but "time" and "nine" are not a
18 true rhyme. Even a dead poet could tell you that.

19   My mom says if I spent less time complaining about too much
20 homework and more time actually doing it, it wouldn't take me so
21 long. Now that is ridiculous. I have to talk about my assignments
22 before I begin — to get myself geared up for them. You can't just
23 tackle a stack of homework without preparing yourself.

24   After many months of overload by Mrs. Wetherby, I'm something
25 of an expert on homework. I've even developed some strategies to
26 make it easier to get started. Here is my sure-fire list of how to get
27 ready to do your homework:

28   One: Fix a good snack. By "good" I do not mean nutritious. I
29 mean something to sustain you when you're in the depths of the Civil
30 War. Something like nachos or chocolate-covered peanuts.

31   Two: Turn on some music. Don't use soft background music. It's
32 hard enough to keep your eyes open while reading Mrs. Wetherby's
33 assignments without playing sleep-inducing ballads. Get some hard
34 rock or hip hop; something to jar your nerves and make you snap your
35 fingers. It will help you stay awake.

1   Three: Telephone your best friend, to solicit sympathy. If you're
2 lucky, your friend will have homework, too. It is easier to study if you
3 know your buddies are suffering at the same time. As Mrs. Wetherby
4 would say, "Misery loves company."

5   Four: Try on at least three outfits and decide which one you'll wear
6 to school tomorrow. You can't concentrate on Valley Forge if you're
7 worried about whether your favorite red shirt needs to be washed, so
8 get your clothes ready before you open a book.

9   Once you've fixed a snack, turned on some music, called your
10 friend, and laid out tomorrow's clothes, you should be able to actually
11 start your homework — unless your red shirt has a rip in the sleeve.
12 In that case, heed Mrs. Wetherby's advice, and take a stitch in time.

2. The Tooth Fairy Forgot

1   When I was little, I loved the Tooth Fairy. Even though I never saw
2   her, she was one of my favorite beings. I imagined her with sparkly
3   wings and tiny silver shoes.

4   Whoever thought up the Tooth Fairy was a genius. A little kid whose
5   tooth has ached for a couple of days, and whose tongue is sore from
6   constantly wiggling that tooth back and forth, back and forth, and who
7   is then scared witless by discovering blood in his mouth could easily be
8   a total wreck.

9   Instead the kid is told that the Tooth Fairy will take away the no-
10 longer-needed tooth and leave money under his pillow. The kid can
11 exchange a bloody old tooth for cash. How cool is that? Instead of being
12 freaked out, the kid is happy. He's ecstatic! He can't wait to lose more
13 teeth.

14   I remember waking up on mornings after I'd lost a tooth and
15 sticking my hand under my pillow, feeling for the quarters I was sure I'd
16 find. I always got two quarters. Fifty cents. Not exactly a fortune, yet it
17 was such important money — magical money, because it appeared in
18 the night while I was sleeping.

19   One time the Tooth Fairy forgot to come. I woke as usual and thrust
20 my hand under the pillow, but instead of quarters, my fingers found the
21 small plastic bag with my tooth inside it, the one I'd put there the night
22 before. Had the Tooth Fairy forgotten to take my tooth when she left the
23 money? Or was there something wrong with this tooth and the Fairy had
24 rejected it?

25   I lifted the pillow and examined the sheet beneath it. No quarters. I
26 looked on the floor, in case I had knocked the money off while I slept. I
27 got down and peered under the bed, but all I saw was a pencil, a
28 bookmark, a pair of shoelaces, and a whole lot of dust bunnies.

29   I trudged downstairs to breakfast, barely able to contain my tears.

1   "What's wrong?" my mom asked.

2   "The Tooth Fairy didn't take my tooth."

3   Mom got an odd look on her face. "Probably," she said, "the Tooth
4   Fairy was just really busy last night and didn't have time for all of the
5   places she needed to go."

6   My lower lip trembled as I whispered my fear, "Maybe she doesn't
7   want my tooth."

8   Mom assured me that the Tooth Fairy never refuses to take a child's
9   tooth. Never. Even if it has a cavity in it. Even if the kid forgets to floss.

10   I wanted to believe her, but I was nervous all day. What if I was the
11   first kid in the history of the world to have a tooth turned down by the
12   Tooth Fairy? What if I left that bag under my pillow night after night for
13   months, and it was always there in the morning? Do old teeth start to
14   stink after a while?

15   I opened the little bag and examined my tooth. It didn't appear to
16   be any different than the others I'd lost. Maybe that was the problem.
17   Maybe the Tooth Fairy already had a gazillion teeth identical to mine and
18   didn't have any use for another one.

19   What if the Tooth Fairy had retired? Maybe she had quit her job and
20   moved to Florida, like my grandpa did.

21   It took me a long time to fall asleep that night — but the next
22   morning, I found a dollar bill under my pillow.

23   "Paper money!" I yelled. "The Tooth Fairy left me a whole dollar!"

24   "The Tooth Fairy probably left more than usual because you had to
25   wait an extra night for her to come," Mom said.

26   "Maybe the Tooth Fairy has raised her rates!" I said. "Probably from
27   now on she'll always leave me a dollar."

28   "Don't count on it," Mom said.

29   Mom was right. The next time I lost a tooth, it was back to the old
30   fifty-cent routine.

31   When the last of my baby teeth fell out, I felt sad. It meant no more
32   money under my pillow; no more magical midnight visits from a small
33   creature with sparkly wings and tiny silver shoes. Even though I never
34   saw her, I miss the Tooth Fairy.

3. Doggie Delights

1   My family took our dog, Charlie, along when we went to the
2 beach. We imagined Charlie running on the sand, his ears flapping
3 and his tail streaming out behind him. We thought Charlie would
4 plunge into the water to retrieve sticks. He would love it, we thought.
5   Well, we got part of it right. Charlie did like going to the beach,
6 but the part he loved most was rolling on a dead fish. What a stink!
7 Before we realized what he was doing, he was thoroughly saturated
8 with dead fish smell. Then he refused to go in the water. We thought
9 the waves would wash at least some of the smell out, but Charlie
10 would have none of it. No matter how many sticks I threw into the
11 water, he refused to fetch them. He just kept running back to that fish
12 and flopping down on top of it and wriggling around in delight. I
13 swear, that dog actually grinned.
14   Finally my dad dug a hole in the sand and we buried the fish, but
15 Charlie kept rolling where the fish used to be. Then he dug up the
16 carcass and started carrying it around in his teeth. That's when Mom
17 decided we were going home early.
18   Our car will never smell the same.
19   The ill-fated trip to the beach isn't the only time that Charlie
20 proved socially inept. Once when Mom entertained her book club at
21 our house, she had all the ladies put their coats on her bed. Charlie
22 saw this heap of coats and decided it would be a comfy place to take
23 a nap. That wouldn't have been so bad; dog fur brushes off pretty
24 easily. Unfortunately, before he found the coats, Charlie had gotten
25 into the garbage, and while he was on the bed, he threw up.
26   Mom heard the retching sound and rushed into the bedroom,
27 trailed by her guests, just in time to see the action. Charlie managed
28 to hit six different coats and two purses, which couldn't have been
29 easy. Mom and the other ladies screamed. Charlie leaped down and

1 hid under the bed. I made the mistake of laughing, which got me the
2 happy task of helping to clean up the mess. One good thing about
3 that evening was that for some reason the ladies didn't have much
4 appetite, so there were plenty of leftover cookies at the end of the
5 meeting.
6   One of Charlie's finest moments came when Dad returned a
7 library book that Charlie had chewed on. Dad explained what had
8 happened and offered to pay for the book. The librarian laughed so
9 hard she cried when she saw the book's title: *How to Train Your*
10 *Puppy.* "I guess it didn't work," she said.
11   There was also the time Charlie ate Mom's paycheck, and the
12 Christmas Eve when he ripped the wrapping off a box of candy, ate
13 the candy, and then ran up and down the front of the sofa, wiping the
14 chocolate off his whiskers.
15   With all of the trouble Charlie gets into, you might wonder why
16 our family keeps him. That's easy: we love him. He's part of the family,
17 and he's one of us, no matter what he does.
18   Charlie's never done anything bad intentionally. He didn't plan to
19 root around in the kitchen garbage and eat eggshells and throw up on
20 those coats.
21   So when Charlie makes a mess or does something wrong, we
22 remind ourselves that he's only acting like a dog. Then we pet him
23 and play with him and try to wear him out so that he doesn't get into
24 more mischief.

4. I Need a Cellphone

1   The worst part about being a kid is the helpless feeling that comes
2   from wanting something, knowing you really need it, and not being
3   able to have it. I want a cellphone. I *need* a cellphone. I absolutely
4   positively must have a cellphone or I will be a social outcast forever.
5   I am the only person in my grade who doesn't have a cellphone. I am
6   probably the only fourteen-year-old in the whole country who doesn't
7   have a cellphone.

8   The reason I don't have one is that my parents are completely
9   and totally paranoid. They think cellphones cause brain cancer. They're
10 convinced that twenty years from now all the people who are
11 currently walking around with phones stuck on their ears will be
12 sprouting tumors and undergoing chemo.

13 I tried to tell them a phone is a safety device. I said it's a way for
14 me to call for help if I need it, but my dad pointed toward a cluster of
15 kids in front of the school, all talking on their phones, and said, "The
16 nine-one-one lines must be overloaded if all those kids are calling for
17 help."

18 All right, so maybe it isn't only a safety measure. Maybe I'd also
19 like to talk to my friends once in a while. What's wrong with that?

20 Statistically, I'm sure there's a way bigger chance that I'll get
21 mugged on the street because I don't have a ride home and no way
22 to call than there is that I'll get brain cancer from calling for someone
23 to pick me up. Of course, I can't prove that. But my parents can't
24 prove their theory, either.

25 I saved up my babysitting money so that I could pay for a phone
26 myself, but even then my retro parents said no.

27 It isn't only cellphones that my parents don't trust. It's also
28 microwave ovens. My mom says, "Do not put your hand in a
29 microwave oven until thirty seconds after it stops." She thinks the

1 little microwaves continue to bounce around in there after the timer
2 beeps, and she doesn't want them to nuke my hands because if they
3 do, then in twenty years not only will I have a tumor on my ear from
4 the phone but another one on my hand from the microwave.

5 I won't even start on what they think happens to a person who
6 sleeps under an electric blanket.

7 If my parents had their way, the government would require
8 warning labels for everything. Candy is hazardous to your health. Do
9 not consume even one chocolate bar unless you want to be obese for
10 the rest of your life.

11 I suppose I should be glad that my parents love me enough to
12 worry about me. I know there are kids whose parents don't care what
13 they eat, where they go, or who they hang out with. But I wonder if
14 it's possible to care too much?

15 My family needs a mediator, like they have in small claims court —
16 someone who could negotiate a balance between what I want and
17 what my parents think I should have. I could give up chocolate bars
18 in return for a cellphone. It isn't going to happen, though, because I'm
19 the only one who thinks we have a problem.

20 Dad and Mom say when I'm grown up, I can make my own
21 decisions, but until then I have to abide by theirs. So take a good look
22 at me. I'm like a seventy-eight r.p.m. record, or a manual typewriter.
23 You may never again see a kid my age who doesn't have a cellphone.

5. Grampa's Eyes

1   Grampa had the best ideas. "Let's build a fort," he'd say, or "Who
2   wants blackberry pie for breakfast?" I always knew when he was
3   going to suggest something fun, because his eyes sparkled before he
4   spoke the words.

5   Grampa's eyes always twinkled when he joked. Even if he
6   pretended to be serious, those laughing brown eyes gave him away.

7   When we played card games, Grampa asked, "Do you want me
8   to shuffle?" I always said, "Yes." He didn't mix up the cards; he stood,
9   put his head down, hunched his shoulders, and moved slowly around
10   the table without lifting his feet off the floor. Even when I knew it was
11   coming, the shuffle trick made me laugh every time.

12   Grampa didn't like to sit around and do nothing. I don't like to sit
13   around and do nothing, either. Maybe that's why we were pals. When
14   I got bored, Grampa's eyes would look thoughtful, and then he'd
15   suggest we go for a hike, or build a birdhouse, or make root beer
16   floats.

17   Grampa liked baseball. I like baseball, too. We watched games on
18   TV, and sometimes we went to the ballpark. Grampa never cared how
19   loud I yelled, and he never left before the game ended, no matter
20   how many innings it took, or how lopsided the score was. Grampa
21   believed in giving everyone a chance to make up for their mistakes:
22   baseball teams and kids.

23   Grampa liked to hold me on his lap. After I got too big to sit on
24   other laps, I still sometimes sat on Grampa's. His lap was just right for
25   snuggling and I never felt babyish sitting there because Gramma
26   sometimes sat on his lap, too, and she's the oldest person I know.

27   Grampa hugged me each time I got to his house, and he hugged
28   me when I left. Sometimes if I wanted to go past him, he blocked my
29   way and said I had to pay a hug toll before I could get by. His eyes

1   smiled at me when he said that, so I knew he would have let me by
2   even if I didn't want to hug him. But I always did.
3   When I stayed overnight, I got in bed with Gramma and Grampa
4   in the morning. We sat propped up with pillows, while Grampa read
5   the comics out loud. Grampa's favorite was *Peanuts*. My favorite was
6   *Peanuts*, too, especially when it was about Snoopy.
7   Grampa played the games nobody else wanted to play. Once
8   when I was about eight, we spent one whole afternoon playing
9   restaurant. Grampa was the customer; I was the waiter. We used toy
10 plates and fake food, and I wrote his order in a notebook. Grampa
11 ordered fried toenails and dandelion sandwiches. He asked for
12 chopped feathers on his pizza. His brown eyes grew wide with
13 pretend shock when I said my restaurant did not serve eraser-flavored
14 ice cream.
15   Another day we played garage sale. I put price tags on all my toys
16 and spread them all over the living room and then he pretended to
17 buy what I had for sale. We used play money and he gladly paid five
18 hundred dollars for my ratty old stuffed cat because he knew it was
19 my favorite toy. At the end of the sale, we took off all the price tags
20 and Grampa gave back everything he had bought.
21   When Grampa looked at me, there was a special glow in his eyes.
22 Gramma said the glow was lovelight. It was there when he looked at
23 her, too. If you see lovelight in someone's eyes, you know that person
24 would do anything in the world for you because you're so special.
25 Lovelight makes you want to try hard and do your best. It makes you
26 want to be worthy.
27   I cried when Grampa died, and I still cry sometimes when I
28 remember him and the fun we had. I wish I could watch a baseball
29 game with him or read the comics together in bed. If he came to my
30 restaurant today, I'd pretend to serve anything he ordered, even an
31 octopus milkshake.
32   Now when I play cards with Gramma, I ask her if she wants me to
33 shuffle and she says, "Yes." Then I imitate Grampa shuffling around the
34 table, and we both laugh.
35   Last night Gramma and I watched the sunset together. As fat pink

1   clouds tinged with gold bumped across the sky I said, "I wish Grampa
2   could see this sunset. I miss him."

3   Gramma said, "I miss him, too, but maybe his eyes are seeing this
4   sunset."

5   I waited for her to explain.

6   "Many years ago," she told me, "Grampa signed up to be an
7   organ and tissue donor. He said when he died, he wanted any usable
8   body parts to be passed along to someone who needed them."
9   Gramma put her hand on my shoulder. "The corneas from Grampa's
10   eyes were transplanted into someone who couldn't see," she told me.
11   "Do you know what the corneas are?"

12   I shook my head, no.

13   She said, "The cornea is the clear, transparent part that covers the
14   pupil and the iris."

15   "Who got Grampa's corneas?" I asked.

16   Gramma didn't know. But she did know that the surgery was
17   successful.

18   I hope whoever received the corneas from Grampa's eyes is using
19   them to watch baseball and play cards and build birdhouses. I wonder
20   if the twinkle in Grampa's eyes got transplanted, too, and the
21   lovelight.

22   Grampa had the best ideas, such as eating blackberry pie for
23   breakfast, and making a fort — and donating the corneas from his
24   eyes to someone who couldn't see.

6. Toto Tells the Truth about Oz

1   My name is Toto. I'm a cairn terrier, and I'm the dog from the
2   book and movie, *The Wizard of Oz*. I'm here to set the record straight
3   about what really happened when Dorothy and I got caught in that
4   tornado and ended up in the Land of Oz. Everyone thinks Dorothy
5   was the clever one in that story, but Dorothy and the Cowardly Lion
6   and the Scarecrow and the Tin Man would never had made it if I
7   hadn't been there.
8   For one thing, none of them had the slightest sense of direction.
9   Every time they stopped for any reason, they forgot which way they
10   had been headed. They knew they were supposed to follow the
11   yellow brick road, but half the time they started following it the wrong
12   way, going back where they'd been instead of on toward the Wizard.
13   I had to bark and run forward until they followed me. It was tough
14   work, being the leader of that pack.
15   The Lion kept cowering and hiding behind trees at the slightest
16   sound, even though I told him I would protect him. The straw man
17   kept flopping over, and I'd have to nudge him with my nose to get
18   him upright again. The Tin Man squeaked so much it hurt my ears. I
19   finally sniffed out an oil can so that Dorothy could un-rust him. Of
20   course, after that he smelled like Three-in-One Oil, but that was better
21   than the constant squeaks.
22   Dorothy herself was practically useless. How helpful was it to
23   stand around singing about rainbows when what we really needed
24   was a good sandwich and a bed to sleep in?
25   Yes, if it had been left up to the rest of that group, we might still
26   be dithering along the yellow brick road. Luckily, I was there to urge
27   them onward. When we arrived at our destination, the guard turned
28   Dorothy and the others down flat. In fact, he slammed the door in
29   their faces. Fortunately, I was there. I barked and scratched at the

1   Wizard's door until the guard got tired of listening to me yap and let
2   us in.
3   Of course, I'm the brave one who ran forward and pulled down
4   the curtain that the so-called Wizard was hiding behind. Even the
5   movie version shows that, but even so, the Munchkins all cheered,
6   "Hooray for Dorothy!" instead of, "Hooray for Toto!"
7   To be fair, I know that Dorothy does love me. It's just that she
8   underestimates my worth. The whole movie is about how wonderful
9   it is that the lion gets courage, and the straw man gets a brain, and
10   the Tin Man gets a heart. Nobody seems to notice that I had all of
11   those attributes to begin with.
12   And it's a good thing I did. My brain led us to Oz, my courage
13   uncovered the Wizard's trickery, and my heart showed the others
14   what true friendship is. Wouldn't you think, at the very least, the good
15   witch Glinda would have provided some dog biscuits?

7. The Pedometer

1   My grandma gave me, and everyone in my family, a pedometer.
2   It hooks on my pants and counts how many steps I take. Grandma
3   tries to take at least five thousand steps every day to stay healthy, and
4   she thought the rest of us might be motivated to be more active if we
5   also kept track of how many steps we took.

6   It seemed a harmless enough idea. It even sounded kind of fun.
7   The first day, I clipped the pedometer to my waistband when I got
8   dressed. Every so often I checked the numbers, but they didn't seem
9   to add up very quickly. I discovered it is eighty-two steps from my
10   front door to the bus stop. It is another sixty steps from the bus to the
11   door of the school, and forty-eight more to my classroom. Add all that
12   to the one hundred and twelve steps I took inside my house, before
13   I left for the bus, and I had a total of three hundred and two steps from
14   the time I got up to the time I reached my desk. From then until lunch,
15   I only added eleven steps, going to the pencil sharpener and back.

16   Things improved in the afternoon because we played kickball in
17   P.E. Wow! That put more than eight hundred steps on my pedometer.

18   That night after dinner, Mom asked everyone to read how many
19   steps they'd taken. My total was a pathetic sixteen hundred twenty-
20   nine. That's less than one-third of what my grandma does every day.
21   How can a seventy-year-old granny be three times more active than
22   me?

23   "Maybe you should walk to school, instead of taking the bus,"
24   Mom suggested.

25   "Ride your bike or roller skate in the afternoon instead of playing
26   computer games," Dad chimed in.

27   That's how it started: the great attempt to make me an active kid.
28   At first I resisted, but they kept after me. Every night I had to
29   announce my pedometer reading and listen to suggestions of how I

1   could up the numbers.

2   After a few days, I got tired of being nagged and decided I'd

3   show them. The next morning, I walked to school: two thousand

4   thirty-one steps. At lunch, instead of gossiping with my friends, I

5   played basketball. Another four hundred and sixteen steps. After I

6   walked home from school, I had a snack and then put the leash on our

7   dog, Otter, and took her around the neighborhood. Otter loved it, and

8   I added another one thousand, two hundred and fourteen steps.

9   When Mom asked for the daily tally that evening, I had a total of five

10   thousand eight hundred and ninety-two steps. More than Grandma!

11   The next day I decided to try to break six thousand. I walked to

12   school and back, played kickball during P.E., took Otter to the park,

13   and then added a bike ride. Just before dinner time, I looked at my

14   pedometer: I still needed another four hundred steps to reach my

15   goal, so I put some music on my iPod and danced around my room.

16   I did it! My tally that day was six thousand and eighty-two. I called

17   Grandma to tell her, and she said it sounded as if she'd better hustle

18   or I would leave her in the dust.

19   Now here's the odd part: I started this to get my parents off my

20   back about being active, but then I discovered that I really do feel

21   better when I move more. I don't always make it to six thousand,

22   especially if it rains and I take the bus to school. But I've found lots of

23   ways to make my numbers higher. Instead of sitting like a lump to

24   watch TV, I get up during every commercial and walk around. One of

25   my friends and I meet at a skateboard park a couple of times a week,

26   to practice our moves, and I signed up for the track team.

27   I'd tell you more, but my best pal, Otter, is waiting for me to take

28   her out. We're trying for seven thousand.

8. Good-bye, Old Jeans

1   My favorite jeans are gone. I feel as if I've lost my best friend. I
2 had those jeans for at least three years, and I wore them every single
3 day unless they were being washed. That happened only when my
4 mom sneaked into my room while I was asleep, grabbed the jeans,
5 and threw them in the washer.

6   Other people did not understand about those jeans. My mother
7 would say, "Just wear a different pair of jeans. Wear those nice new
8 ones that I bought on sale."

9   What she didn't understand is that the nice new jeans were stiff
10 and uncomfortable and dark blue. When I had those new jeans on, I
11 was aware of them.

12   My good jeans, on the other hand, were soft and faded with holes
13 worn in the knees. They fit my body as if they had been designed
14 especially for me. They were comfy and flexible, and I hardly knew I
15 had them on. Stepping into those old jeans was like spending the day
16 with a friend I'd known since kindergarten.

17   Sometimes I had to get dressed up to go to an event where my
18 old jeans, according to my parents, were not appropriate. My Aunt
19 Susan's wedding, for example, and the time my family went to an
20 opera. On those occasions I was forced to wear something other than
21 my favorite jeans, but as soon as I got home, I raced to my room,
22 pulled off the dressy clothes I had on, and stepped happily into my
23 comfy old jeans.

24   My mom had told me a year ago that my favorite jeans were
25 wearing out, but I refused to listen. They could hang from my hips in
26 shreds and I would still wear them.

27   Unfortunately, besides wearing thin, my jeans got too small. Or,
28 rather, I got too big. They started to feel tight a year ago, but I
29 continued to stuff myself into them. For the last few months, I had to

1 hold my breath and suck my stomach in when I put them on. Last
2 week, even when I did that, I was no longer able to pull the zipper
3 up. They were also too short.
4   "Face it," my mother said. "Those ratty old jeans don't fit you any
5 more." I knew she was glad. She had told me many times she was
6 sick of seeing me dressed like I should be standing on the corner of
7 the freeway holding a sign that said, "Will Work for Food."
8   Reluctantly, I acknowledged that my favorite jeans no longer fit.
9 Mom held out her hand to take them. "What are you going to do with
10 them?" I asked.
11   "Throw them in the garbage," she said. "They're too worn to
12 donate to a charity."
13   I refused to see my beloved jeans end up in the trash can.
14   Instead, I decided to have a funeral and bury them in my back
15 yard.
16   "You're *what?*" my sister cried when I invited her to attend. Then
17 she shook her head and declared I had just proved what she had
18 always suspected, that I was seriously challenged in the IQ
19 department.
20   So I held the funeral by myself. I dug a hole and laid my jeans in
21 it. I lit the candle stub that was left from my jack-o-lantern. I even
22 wrote a poem, which I recited after I had covered the jeans with dirt.
23 My poem went like this:
24   "Goodbye, old jeans;
25   I'll miss you so.
26   I wish you didn't
27   Have to go.
28   I loved you long,
29   With all my might,
30   But in the end,
31   You were too tight."
32   *(Sniff. Wipe eyes.)*
33   Sorry. I'm too sad to continue.

9. One Vote

1   My school held elections yesterday to decide our class officers,
2   but I didn't vote. To make it like a real election, we had to vote on our
3   own time instead of during class. I didn't vote in the morning because
4   I overslept and barely made it to my first period class. During lunch, I
5   finished a book report that was due, and after school I got talking with
6   my friends and forgot about voting. I remembered after I got home,
7   and I could have gone back, but I didn't. I figured my one vote
8   wouldn't make any difference. I knew who would win anyway.

9   There were three people running for class president, and we were
10   required to attend an assembly last week where each one of them
11   told what they would do if they were elected.

12   The first candidate was Joanie, and if I could have walked out of
13   the auditorium, I would have. The faculty should provide barf bags if
14   they're going to make us listen to her. *(Pretends to be Joanie.)* "I am
15   just so, like, totally honored to be, like, nominated for President. If I'm
16   elected I'll, like, make sure we have, you know, less homework and
17   more pep assemblies, way more pep assemblies, because that's what
18   school should be about, right? It should be about having fun together,
19   right? And, like, cheering for our teams and stuff. Go, Tigers!"

20   All of her ditzy friends yelled and clapped as if she'd made the
21   best speech of the year. I couldn't believe it.

22   Roland spoke next. His ideas were OK, but he seriously needs to
23   take a class in public speaking. *(Speaks in a monotone.)* "We need a
24   student representative on the School Board because as it is now the
25   adults make all of the decisions but it's our school and our lives that
26   get affected so I'd like to see the class president be appointed to the
27   School Board and if I'm elected I'll attend all of their meetings and
28   make our opinions known."

29   The last candidate, and clearly the only qualified one, was Tyler.

1   He had a three part agenda. One: Give extra credit for community
2   service, as a way to encourage students to help those who are less
3   fortunate. Two: Offer after-school tutorials where kids who are
4   struggling in a subject can get help with their homework. Three: Start
5   a district-wide recycling program so that all the paper, juice cans, and
6   other recyclable materials quit going into the garbage.

7   Tyler was terrific. He spoke clearly and stayed around to answer
8   questions. He would make a great class president.

9   There are one hundred and eighty-four kids in my grade. Only
10 ninety-eight of them voted! I thought everyone would vote, but they
11 didn't. I assumed my vote didn't matter because this election was
12 bound to be a landslide for Tyler.

13 I was wrong. Roland got five votes, which is four more than I
14 would have expected, assuming he voted for himself. Tyler got forty-
15 six votes, and Joanie got forty-seven. If it had been a tie, there would
16 have been another election with only those two candidates, and I'll
17 bet all of the people who didn't vote, like me, would have made sure
18 to cast their ballot. Since Joanie's friends all showed up the first time,
19 I have no doubt most of those additional votes would have been for
20 Tyler. He would have won. He should have won.

21 Instead, I'm stuck with Joanie as class president. And it's my own
22 fault for not voting.

10. Fan Letter to a Favorite Author

1   Dear Favorite Author:

2   I love your books. They are the best books in the world. I love
3   them so much that I won't read anybody else's books, but I've already
4   read everything you've written, and I need something new to read,
5   so please write faster.

6   Please send me an autographed book. Better yet, send me signed
7   copies of all of your books. Send a picture of you, too, and a poster,
8   and some bookmarks. I want all this stuff so I can show it to my friends
9   and make them jealous.

10   I have an idea for your next book, and I won't charge you
11   anything for it. You can write about me! Wouldn't that be cool? You
12   could use my name, and there could be this stupid younger brother
13   named Jason and a best friend named Kelly. Oh, and use Madison
14   School as the setting. If you need to do some research, you could
15   come to visit my class. I don't know the school's address, but I'm sure
16   you can find it on the Internet.

17   To return the favor of such a great idea, you could dedicate your
18   next book to me. I noticed that all your books are dedicated to people
19   you know, such as your husband or your children. One is dedicated
20   to your editor, and one is even dedicated to your dogs. Well, what
21   about me? I'm sure you have a nice family and a good editor and
22   great dogs, but where would you be without readers? Nowhere!
23   Since I am your number one fan, I think you should dedicate the next
24   book to me. I'm putting my return address on the envelope; you can
25   mail all my free copies there.

26   I need you to answer a few questions because I'm doing a book
27   report on your wonderful book, *Danny's Dangerous Pine Cones*,
28   which, by the way, is my favorite book of all time. I have read it
29   thirteen times. So here are my questions:

1   One: Where does this book take place?

2   Two: Who are the characters?

3   Three: What is the problem?

4   Four: How is the problem resolved?

5   Five: How many pages does this book have?

6   Six: What message do you think the author wanted to send?

7   Answer these questions right away because my book report is

8 due tomorrow morning.

9   Your number one fan,

10   _____ *(Name)*

11. The Day I Was a Dog

1 The day I turned into a dog I didn't tell anyone. At the age of five,
2 I believed in fairies and magic, so the transformation didn't seem
3 extraordinary to me, and I kept it secret. Until now, I've never told
4 anyone what happened the day I became a dog.

5 I was digging in my sandbox when a flat-faced dog the color of
6 hot chocolate began sniffing around the back fence. "Hi, dog," I said.
7 The dog stopped sniffing and stared at me through the wire. Our eyes
8 locked as if we were friends from long ago who were surprised to find
9 each other. Recognition arced briefly between us, and then I was the
10 dog, sniffing at the leaves that huddled at the base of the fence, and
11 he was a little girl shoveling sand into a bright blue pail.

12 I can't explain how this happened, or why. I only know that I
13 suddenly had four short legs, a tail that curled over my back, and
14 breath that smelled like last week's meat loaf. When my nanny said,
15 "Shoo! Get out of here, dog," I trotted away, thrilled with my new
16 independence. I went to the corner, crossed the street, and kept
17 going. When I came to Pearson's Bakery, I saw the pastries and cakes
18 in the window, and realized that if I didn't change back into myself
19 soon, I would miss Suzie Tarrow's birthday party and the chance to
20 stuff myself with chocolate cake and ice cream.

21 I ran back home, stood outside the fence, and barked to get the
22 attention of the girl in the sandbox. "Shoo!" cried Nanny. She reached
23 for a stone, and I realized she was going to throw it at me! Before she
24 did, the girl looked up, our eyes locked, an unseen current zapped
25 between us, and we switched bodies again.

26 I quickly pulled on Nanny's arm. "Don't chase the dog away," I
27 said. "I like him."

28 Nanny dropped the stone. "It's time to wash up," she said, "so
29 you aren't late to your party." I hurried inside without watching to see

1   what the little dog did.

2   When my parents got home that evening, they asked me, as they
3   do every day, "What did you do today? Anything special happen?"

4   I told them I won a prize playing musical chairs, and I told them
5   how Libby spilled orange soda on Mrs. Tarrow's shoes, but I didn't tell
6   them that I had briefly been a dog — because I knew I wanted to do
7   it again and I knew they would tell me not to.

8   Every day for the next week, I spent all my time in the sandbox,
9   hoping the little brown dog would come to the fence. He never did.
10   A big black poodle came once and I tried staring at her, but although
11   she wagged her tail and looked back at me, I stayed where I was —
12   a little girl in a sandbox — and the poodle remained a dog.

13   Next, I begged to go for walks, hoping to see the brown dog.
14   Nanny and I circled the block every morning and every afternoon for
15   a week, but I didn't find the brown dog with the curly tail. Since then,
16   every time I see a dog, I look deep into its eyes, but the magic
17   transformation has never happened again.

18   Even though I was a dog for such a brief time, the experience left
19   me with a sense of kinship. When Nanny was going to throw that
20   stone, the small brown dog couldn't ask her not to; I had to speak for
21   him. Since that day, I've tried to be a voice for the animals. They can't
22   ask for help themselves; they need us to do it for them.

23   I don't recall many things about my early childhood, but I've
24   never forgotten the magical day when I ran on four paws, wagged my
25   tail, and barked.

12. Fatty Patty

1   When my sister was in fifth grade, she started to gain weight. I
2   called her Fatty Patty. Until then, Patty had been a normal-size kid, like
3   me, but then her face gradually puffed out like a chipmunk that is
4   gathering nuts for the winter. She had to buy new clothes in larger
5   sizes.

6   "Hey, Fatty Patty," I said. "Maybe you should try shopping in the
7   maternity department."

8   Looking back, I don't know why I was so mean. At the time, I
9   didn't even realize how cruel it was. I was just teasing my younger
10 sister, zeroing in on what I perceived as her failure.

11   In honesty, I probably did it partly to make myself look good. I'm
12 only one year older than Patty, so there's always been a certain
13 amount of sibling rivalry. Although I love my sister, I like it when she's
14 in trouble and I'm not. I was skinny as a flagpole that year, which
15 made Patty look all the heavier.

16   Midway through the school year, Mom took Patty to our family
17 doctor for a checkup. She had gained twenty-two pounds in seven
18 months; she was the same height as she'd been at her last visit. The
19 doctor said Patty was probably getting ready to have a growth spurt.
20 He said kids often bulk up prior to adding a few inches to their height.
21 He said not to worry.

22   "You're having a growth spurt, all right," I told Patty. "You're
23 growing sideways." I assumed Patty was sneaking food at night, or
24 spending her allowance on candy. That's why people gain weight,
25 right? They eat too much.

26   When the growth spurt didn't start, Mom and Dad took Patty to
27 a pediatrician. He said Patty should have a CAT scan.

28   I was outside riding my bike when Patty got home after the CAT
29 scan. I should have realized something was wrong but I was so eager

27

1   to deliver the one-liner I'd made up that I didn't notice how pale Patty
2   looked or the fact that Mom's eyes were red, as if she'd been crying.

3   "Fatty Patty had a catty," I said.

4   Instead of telling me to shut up, as I expected, my sister looked
5   at me for few seconds, then walked into the house.

6   "Come inside," Mom said. I followed her.

7   Moments later I found out that my sister had a brain tumor. It was
8   pressing on her pituitary gland, which made her hormones go all
9   goofy and caused her to gain weight. It was also next to the optic
10   nerve, and the doctor was surprised Patty hadn't complained of
11   problems with her eyesight. Patty was scheduled for brain surgery at
12   Children's Hospital for the tumor to be removed.

13   That's when I knew what fear felt like … and shame. I learned that
14   dread can creep under your skin and burrow so deep that you can't
15   think of anything except the fact that your sister might have cancer,
16   might go blind, might never get well. What if Patty died?

17   When I thought of all the times I had teased her for gaining
18   weight, I wanted to dig a hole and crawl into it and never come out.
19   How could I have been so clueless?

20   The day of Patty's surgery was the longest day of my life. I took a
21   book to the hospital, but I didn't read it. All I did was wait. That's what
22   we all did — Mom and Dad, and Grandpa and Grandma, and me —
23   for six hours, we waited.

24   Finally, the surgeon came out and said the operation was over and
25   that Patty would be fine. I felt such relief that I half expected to float
26   up to the ceiling.

27   Although we had to wait for biopsy results to be positive, the
28   surgeon said he was sure Patty's tumor was not cancer. He had been
29   able to get it all out. Every trace. There was no damage to the optic
30   nerve. Never had so much good news been delivered in so short a
31   time.

32   Patty stayed in the hospital for six days. She missed the last two
33   months of fifth grade, but she made up the work during the summer.
34   It's been over a year since her surgery; she still has to go for checkups
35   every three months. So far, the tumor has not come back.

1   My sister lost the puffiness and returned to a normal weight.
2 She's growing again. She's the same old Patty, as if none of this had
3 happened.
4   I'm different, though. The kid who felt superior by putting
5 someone else down is gone. The one who whispered "Fatty Patty" no
6 longer makes hurtful jokes. Not that I'm perfect. I still tease Patty now
7 and then — but never about something she can't control. I wouldn't
8 call her Fatty Patty if she weighed three hundred pounds. I'll never say
9 Fatty Patty, or any other mean joke, again.
10   My sister got sick, but her surgery changed me.

13. The Last Piece of the Puzzle

1   My sister makes me so angry. We both like to work jigsaw
2   puzzles, and we're both good at it, even though we use different
3   approaches. I'm a color person. I look to see what color a missing
4   piece should be, and then I search for pieces of that color.

5   Angie's a shape person. She looks for knobs to fit into openings,
6   or outside pieces that have straight edges. She's always saying she
7   needs a piece with two knobs and a hole, or something like that,
8   whereas I'm more likely to say I need a piece that's brown on one
9   side and green on the other.

10   You might think that our separate methods would mean that we
11   would be a good team when it comes to working puzzles. We
12   probably would be, if Angie wasn't so totally selfish.

13   There is something very satisfying about putting in the last piece
14   of the puzzle. Sometimes, with a big puzzle that has several hundred
15   pieces, it takes us a week or more to put it together. After all those
16   hours of searching for pieces and watching the picture take shape,
17   when you finally drop the final puzzle piece into place, it's a feeling
18   of accomplishment: Wow! I did it!

19   The trouble in my family is that nobody but Angie ever gets that
20   feeling because every time we work a puzzle, she sneaks a piece into
21   her pocket, or she sits on it, or she drops it down her shoe. In other
22   words, she hides it where no one else will know about it. That way
23   she knows she will always be the one to put in the last piece.

24   Besides depriving me of the chance to find the last piece, she also
25   causes me to waste a ton of time looking for the piece that she has
26   squirreled away. I used to hunt until I had eye strain and then declare
27   that a certain piece must be missing. Maybe the dog ate it, I would
28   say, or it accidentally got sucked into the vacuum cleaner.

29   After a few times of Angie whipping out that elusive piece at the

1 very end, I got smart. Now, if I spend a couple of minutes
2 unsuccessfully searching for a piece and don't find it, I glare at Angie
3 and demand that she put back the piece she's hiding. She always
4 denies it, of course. Once I held her down and sat on her while I
5 looked in her pockets. She screamed so loud our parents came
6 running into the room, and then I got in trouble even though I found
7 the puzzle piece in Angie's pocket.

8   I received dire warnings about what would happen if I did not quit
9 picking on my sister, so I decided to beat her at her own game. When
10 she left the puzzle to go to the bathroom, I sneaked a piece into my
11 shoe. Then, when we were getting close to finishing the puzzle, I sat
12 with my hand covering that space so Angie didn't notice the piece
13 that was missing.

14   When the whole puzzle was done except for the place under my
15 hand and one more piece, Angie grinned, lifted up the cushion on her
16 chair and plucked out what she thought was the last piece of the
17 puzzle. She stuck it in, then smirked triumphantly at me. I knew she
18 was waiting for me to holler at her. Instead, I moved my hand.

19   "Hmmmm," I said. "It looks like there's still one piece that we
20 need to find." Angie's eyes grew big, and she began frantically
21 looking around on the floor. While she did that, I removed the final
22 piece from my shoe. "Here it is," I said, and I pushed the piece into
23 the gap in the puzzle.

24   If you were within five miles of my house that day, I'm sure you
25 heard her yelling. "No fair!" she screeched. "You cheated! You hid that
26 piece on purpose, just so you could put it in last."

27   "So?" I asked. "You do that every time."

28   Angie glared at me before she stomped off to her room.

29   The next time we work a puzzle, she'll probably still sneak a piece
30 off the table and hide it somewhere. But from now on, she'll never be
31 sure that it's the last piece.

14. Is It Good for Me or Not?

1   I wish the scientists would make up their minds about what's
2 good for us to eat and what isn't. Just when I think I know, they
3 change their minds.

4   Take coffee, for instance. "Coffee will stunt your growth," my dad
5 warned. "Coffee's bad for your health," my mom said, and they
6 refused to let me have even one sip. They drank it every morning, but
7 I couldn't have any.

8   Of course, any kid covets what is forbidden, so whenever I could,
9 I spent my allowance at Starbucks. I was already one of the tallest kids
10 in my class, so I figured if the coffee stunted my growth, it was no big
11 deal. It took awhile before I actually liked the taste of coffee, but I
12 liked doing what adults do, so I drank it anyway, and eventually I
13 learned to enjoy it.

14   I continued to grow, and I think maybe it's a good thing I sneaked
15 all those lattes. Without them, I might be some sort of giant. I still
16 worried, though, that the coffee might be bad for my health. I like
17 cappuccinos, and I adore mochas, but I don't want to be sick.

18   Then, out of the blue came a report from Harvard researchers
19 that, guess what? Coffee is actually good for us! It lowers the risk of
20 colon cancer, Parkinson's disease, and diabetes. It's a mood booster
21 and may even prevent cavities!

22   Next, came the stunning report that dark chocolate can be
23 beneficial for your heart. What great news! Something I love to eat is
24 actually good for me! All those years when my mom rationed out my
25 Halloween candy were wasted effort.

26   I'm hoping the doctors will soon decide that cheese cures cancer.
27 Cheese currently gets a bad rap. When I was little, my mom used to
28 sprinkle grated cheese on all sorts of food as a way to get me to eat
29 enough protein. She thought cheese was good for me, and I loved

1 the taste. Three-cheese pizza. Yum! Grilled cheese sandwiches: my
2 favorite meal! Then Mom learned that cheese is high in saturated fat,
3 which is bad for your heart, so cheese got banished from the fridge.
4 No more lasagna. No more crackers-and-cheese snacks. Life definitely
5 went downhill.
6   Nobody ever picks on broccoli. Why don't the scientists discover
7 that too much broccoli leads to diabetes and obesity? Why can't we
8 have warning labels that say broccoli is potentially dangerous to our
9 health? But, no. The researchers, who seem determined to take the
10 joy out of eating, insist that broccoli is safe and nutritious and will help
11 prevent cancer and heart attacks and probably ingrown toenails, too.
12   Don't brownies prevent any disease? How about banana splits?
13 They're good for my mental health, that's for sure, but nobody seems
14 to care about that.
15   I'm waiting for the happy announcement that new research
16 proves that chocolate-covered cherries are really a health food, and
17 that we all need five or more servings of lemon cream pie every day.
18   I hope it happens soon. I'm getting awfully tired of broccoli.

15. Remembering Little Rock

1   They spit at me, the white kids did. Spit, and kicked, and called
2 me names. They tried to block my way so I couldn't walk down the
3 halls. Central High School was their school, they said. A school for
4 white kids. Only now it was my school, too. The law said so. The U.S.
5 Supreme Court said so. President Eisenhower said so. I have as much
6 right as any white person to walk in that door, sit at a desk, and get
7 myself an education.

8   Wouldn't you think by now people would be more tolerant? It's
9 1957, nearly a century since the Civil War ended. You would assume
10 racial discrimination would be over, but you would be wrong.

11   The night before school started, someone pitched a rock through
12 the front window of my house. Mama cried, and Daddy was so angry
13 his hands shook as he read the note that was taped to the rock. I'm
14 not going to repeat what the note said. It was too hateful.

15   The morning of my first day at school, I was scared. I met the
16 other black kids who were starting school that day so that we could
17 drive to school and walk in together. Four ministers, two black and
18 two white, walked with us.

19   We didn't get inside, though. The governor had ordered the
20 National Guard to prevent us from entering. The Guardsmen let the
21 white kids go in, but raised their bayonets when my group
22 approached, so we had to go back home.

23   It was three weeks before the Guard was called off, and then it
24 happened only after a judge warned the governor that he could go
25 to jail if he continued to defy the court's order.

26   On our second attempt to go to school, we had a police escort.
27 They sneaked us in a side entrance so that the mob of a thousand
28 protestors who had gathered in front of the school didn't see us.
29 Since we weren't in sight, the mob attacked some black

newspapermen who were covering the story, beating and kicking them. That would have been me, if I had tried to go in the front door of my own school.

Two days later, President Eisenhower sent federal troops to Little Rock to make sure the law of the land was obeyed.

Mama's brother died fighting for democracy in World War Two, but Mama said when she saw the soldiers there to drive me to school in an Army vehicle, she felt like an American citizen for the first time.

Democracy or not, school was hard that whole year. My locker was vandalized. I got tripped on the stairs, and once two boys stuck me with safety pins. Sometimes the white kids had "stare days" when they all stared at me the whole day, without saying anything. Hate messages were written in lipstick on the bathroom mirrors. When the school had a Christmas program, I wasn't allowed to be in it.

At home, we got anonymous phone calls with threats to burn our house down. The only way we could sleep was to take the phone off the hook.

Day after day I was kicked and harassed. I wonder where so much hate came from. I wonder how otherwise decent people could be so sure that they were superior to me because of their skin color.

Although it was hard being a black student in a formerly white school, I'm glad I did it. I'm proud that I stood up for what was right. Someday, I'll tell my grandchildren what I did. I wonder how many of the kids who spit on me will tell theirs.

16. Roadside Rescue

1   The black dog often stood beside a stop sign at a busy
2 intersection, watching the cars drive by. Sometimes he walked along
3 the side of the road; sometimes he crossed the road, weaving in and
4 out of the traffic.

5   I saw him from the school bus. All the kids watched for him.

6   "There he is!" we cried. "He's still here." We all worried that the
7 dog would dart in front of a car one day and be killed. Many drivers
8 stopped and tried to coax the dog to get in their car, but he wouldn't
9 do it. Sometimes people brought dog food and put it on the side of
10 the road. The dog ate the food, but only after the people who brought
11 it got back in their cars.

12   Chris, who lives near the intersection, decided to rescue the dog.
13 She sat in the grass for hours, talking to the dog and throwing him
14 pieces of food. The dog learned to recognize Chris, and would come
15 when Chris arrived, but always stayed just out of reach. If Chris tried
16 to move closer, the dog growled. Chris named the dog Lucky.

17   One day, Lucky wasn't there. Worried that he was injured, Chris
18 searched for him but didn't find him. When the school bus passed that
19 corner, all the kids grew quiet. We thought for sure Lucky was dead.

20   For two weeks, the dog failed to appear — and then one day
21 Lucky was back, standing by the stop sign, as if he'd never been
22 gone. Chris resumed her rescue efforts. She got a trap from the
23 Humane Society, and baited it with raw meat. Day after day, Lucky
24 ignored the trap.

25   While Chris stood on the side of the road with treats, trying to get
26 Lucky to come, many people stopped. UPS drivers, parents who
27 drove their kids to school, and commuters all pulled over. Some told
28 how they had tried to catch the dog. More than fifty drivers stopped
29 to say they had watched the dog and were worried about him. "I

1 hope you catch him," they said. "Good luck!" Despite the large
2 cheering squad, the black dog refused to get close to Chris, even for
3 treats.

4   Then Chris decided to try a new tactic. Maybe Lucky could learn
5 to fetch and would eventually bring a ball close enough for Chris to
6 touch him. Chris brought a ball and threw it for Lucky. The dog ran to
7 fetch the ball, brought it back, and dropped it just out of Chris's reach.
8 They played for a long time. Although Lucky kept his distance, he
9 clearly liked the game.

10   After several days of playing ball, Lucky grew friendlier. One day
11 he crept up to Chris and took a piece of cheese out of Chris's hand,
12 then quickly darted away. The next day he tugged on Chris's pant leg,
13 wanting to play ball.

14   Chris was making progress, but she didn't want to undo all the
15 good by making a grab for Lucky too soon and spooking him.

16   A woman who lived near the intersection had a large fenced
17 kennel area for her own dogs. She had watched Chris's efforts. When
18 she saw the black dog playing fetch, she got an idea.

19   "Why don't we open the gate to my kennel," she suggested, "and
20 throw your ball inside? Maybe the dog would go in after it."

21   When Chris agreed, the woman shut her own dogs in her house
22 and left the kennel gate open.

23   Chris threw Lucky's ball for a while, moving ever closer to the
24 open door of the neighbor's kennel. Then, holding her breath, she
25 threw the ball into the kennel. When Lucky raced after it, Chris
26 stepped inside, too, and shut the gate behind her. Chris sat down and
27 talked to Lucky who slowly approached, dropped the ball, and then
28 snuggled next to Chris's side. The long ordeal was over.

29   Before Chris took Lucky home, she took him to a veterinary clinic.
30 The vet said Lucky's back right leg had been broken and had not
31 healed properly, but he didn't think it would cause any problems. For
32 a stray, Lucky was in excellent condition.

33   The next day Chris made a sign and posted it at the intersection
34 where Lucky had spent so much time. The sign said: "The Black Dog
35 Is Safe. He's Been Adopted."

1   I cheered when I saw that sign. All the kids on the school bus
2   cheered, and, one at a time, so did hundreds of other people who
3   regularly drove past that corner.
4   This was a true story. Hooray for Chris!

17. The Homecoming Dance

1   Everyone makes a big deal out of Homecoming. I can see why
2   alumnae might want to come back to visit their high school when all
3   their fellow classmates come, so they can see each other, but I fail to
4   understand why it's so important for those of us who are still in
5   school. I'm already here; I see my classmates every day. There's no
6   place to go home *to* so why all the fuss about Homecoming?

7   The pep rally is always entertaining, and the Homecoming football
8   game is fun, especially if it doesn't rain. The band plays, and the
9   cheerleaders work the crowd into a frenzy of school spirit, and at half
10 time the Homecoming Queen and King ride around the field in a
11 convertible.

12 The big problem with Homecoming is the dance. Nearly all of the
13 girls hope to go to the Homecoming dance. What's worse, the girls'
14 mothers hope their daughters will be invited to the Homecoming
15 dance. My mother, for example. She tries not to be obvious, but she
16 can't keep from asking if anyone I know is going to the Homecoming
17 dance.

18 Maybe most of the boys want to go, too, but a lot of them don't
19 want to go badly enough to ask a girl to go with them. Perhaps the
20 mothers of boys don't care if they stay home. The result is that lots of
21 girls who want to go to the dance don't have a date.

22 Unlike Tolo, when the girls invite the boys, the guy has to ask the
23 girl to go to the Homecoming dance. That's just how it is. No
24 exceptions. So if a girl — like me, for example — wants to go to the
25 Homecoming dance, but no guy asks her to go with him, then she's
26 dateless and stuck at home.

27 Or is she? Maybe not. Karrie and I both really wanted to go to the
28 Homecoming dance. We like to dance, and it was the only school
29 dance this year that had a live band instead of a DJ. "Where is it

1   written," Karrie asked, "that we have to go with guys? Why can't we
2   go to the dance together? Let's get a whole group of girls, so it
3   doesn't look as if the two of us are dating each other."

4   I thought about Karrie's idea and decided, why not? If several of
5   us go, we won't feel conspicuous, and there'll always be somebody
6   to dance with or talk to. We decided to do it.

7   That afternoon I made the mistake of telling my mom that I was
8   going to the Homecoming dance. She freaked out because she
9   thought I had a date. "Who are you going with?" she cried. "When
10   did he ask you?" When I told her nobody had asked me, that I had no
11   date, but I was going with Karrie, Megan, Abby, and a few other girls,
12   she seemed stunned. But then she said, "Good for you. Good for you!"

13   She told me she had missed her Homecoming dance when she
14   was my age, because nobody invited her. She said she stayed home
15   and cried that night, and felt like an ugly loser. It seemed unfair that
16   she didn't get to go to a school event that she wanted to attend just
17   because no boy had asked her to be his date. She said she wished she
18   had done what I was going to do.

19   Mom said she was proud of me, and she hoped I would have a
20   great time with my friends at the Homecoming dance.

21   And I did.

18. Wait Till Next Time

1   The next time Melissa Mulney gets smart with me, I know exactly
2 what I'm going to say to her.
3   Unfortunately, Melissa lives next door to me. Just because she's
4 two years older than I am, she thinks she knows everything and I
5 know nothing.
6   For example, last night I was walking my dog past her house, and
7 Melissa came out just as Max was doing his business. Is there
8 anything more embarrassing than standing still and holding a leash
9 while the dog squats? I pretended to be watching an airplane that was
10 flying over. I stared up as if I were a serious student of aircraft, and
11 had no idea what Max was doing at that moment. When he finished,
12 he jumped away from the spot and began tugging on his leash to
13 continue our walk.
14   I glanced at Melissa's house, hoping she had gone back inside.
15 She hadn't. She stood on the front steps, watching me. I took a plastic
16 bag out of my pocket and slipped my hand inside it, but when I
17 looked at the grass, I didn't see Max's deposit. I couldn't remember
18 exactly where he had been. I walked around carefully for a few
19 seconds, staring at the grass, until I finally saw the mound and
20 scooped it into the bag.
21   Melissa said, "Instead of pretending you don't know what your
22 dog is doing, you ought to put the bag on your hand and stand close
23 to him until he finishes. That way you can find it quickly."
24   I mumbled "OK," and hurried off. But the next time Melissa gives
25 me unwanted advice, I will tell her that since I do not plan a career in
26 poop scooping, it isn't necessary for me to take lessons from her.
27   I'll do better on my next encounter with the skateboard demons,
28 too. There are these two guys who ride their skateboards on the
29 sidewalks around my school, and they never — *never* — yield the

1 right-of-way to anyone. Twice now they have come barreling toward
2 me, and I've had to step off the sidewalk to avoid being run into. They
3 never say "Excuse me," or "Sorry," or "Thank you." They just smirk as
4 they roll by. It's clear that they like to intimidate other kids, as if they
5 are all-powerful.
6   Well, I have a plan for next time. I'm going to carry a bag of
7 marbles, and I'll accidentally spill them all over the sidewalk just
8 before the skateboard demons reach me. I'll jump out of the way, and
9 their skateboards will hit all the marbles. We'll see who's smirking
10 then.
11   The next time I fail a math test will be different, too. Instead of
12 meekly promising my teacher that I will study harder, I plan to tell him
13 that if this school district had not started teaching math in such a weird
14 way when I was in first grade, I wouldn't be failing now.
15   My mom, who is a college graduate, can't help me do my
16 homework because she can't figure out the method I'm supposed to
17 use to get the answers. She saw an article in the paper that says more
18 than half of my state's high school graduates fail math on the
19 standardized tests. So I'm not the only one who struggles. Instead of
20 failing half the kids, the school ought to change how they teach math.
21 Do it so we can understand it.
22   There are many other things that I plan to do differently next time,
23 but I'll have to tell you about them later because my time is up.

19. Mornings Are Meant for Sleeping

1   I am not a morning person. My internal clock is programmed to
2 stay up late at night, and to sleep as late as possible in the morning.
3 This condition creates a lot of friction in my family.

4   My mom used to wake me up on school days. Then, ten minutes
5 later, she would wake me up again. If I still wasn't on my feet when
6 she checked a third time, she actually pulled the covers off me and
7 threatened to pour a glass of ice water on my head. That got me
8 moving. Slowly.

9   When school started this year, Mom announced that I was now
10 old enough to take responsibility for getting myself up and ready to
11 leave for school on time. She gave me an alarm clock. In fact, she
12 gave me two alarm clocks. I'm supposed to set the second one for
13 five minutes after the first one, but leave the second one across the
14 room where I can't reach it to turn it off without getting out of bed.

15   There is only one thing more horrible than being jarred awake by
16 an alarm clock, and that is being jarred awake by *two* alarm clocks.
17 On the first day of school, when the first alarm rang, I turned it off and
18 went back to sleep. Then the second one rang ... and rang ... and rang.
19 I put the pillow over my head and my hands over my ears. I thought
20 it would run down and quit after awhile, but no such luck. Finally I
21 staggered over to it and turned it off.

22   I looked longingly at my cozy bed, but I took a deep breath and
23 somehow mustered the energy to get dressed, eat breakfast, and get
24 to the school bus on time. Mom was ecstatic.

25   She wasn't so thrilled the next morning. That time, I got up as
26 soon as the second alarm rang, turned it off, and crawled back in bed.
27 I was sound asleep when she poked her head in my room to say I had
28 five minutes to eat breakfast and get to the bus stop.

29   I didn't make it. Even by skipping breakfast, I couldn't possibly

1 get ready that fast. I did get up, and I ate a bowl of cereal, and then
2 I told Mom I was ready.
3   "Ready for what?" she asked.
4   "For you to drive me to school," I said. "I missed the bus."
5   She shook her head. "You are responsible for getting yourself to
6 school," she told me. "If you chose not to get up in time to catch the
7 bus, you'll have to walk."
8   "Walk!" I said. "It's almost two miles. I'll never get there on time.
9 Besides, it's raining."
10   Mom shrugged and suggested I take an umbrella.
11   I fumed all the way to school. I arrived almost an hour late and
12 discovered I had missed a great assembly about how service dogs get
13 trained. Some of the dogs had been there and anyone who wanted to
14 could pet them.
15   I had missed it, and it was all my mother's fault.
16   That night after I finished my homework, I started watching a
17 movie. "Don't stay up too late," my dad said. "I hear you had trouble
18 getting up this morning." I just glared at him. I was not the least bit
19 sleepy. I went to bed when the movie ended, though, and the next
20 morning when the first alarm went off, I got up, walked to the second
21 alarm and clicked it off before it rang. I stood there for a few seconds,
22 listening to the rain on the roof and resenting my mother. Then I got
23 ready for school. Much as I wanted to snooze a while longer, it wasn't
24 worth walking to school in the rain and missing an assembly.
25   I'm still not a morning person. On weekends, I sleep until noon if
26 I can, but on school days I get up on time. Now that I'm used to it, I
27 like being in charge of myself instead of having Mom nag at me every
28 morning.

20. Heavenly Dimes

1   *(As monologist enters, he bends down briefly, as if picking*
2   *something up off the floor.)*
3   What I'm about to tell you is pretty weird. At first, I wasn't sure I
4   believed it myself.
5   Here's the deal: my grandpa died a couple of years ago, and now
6   my grandma says he sends her dimes from heaven. I know; it sounds
7   wacko, but my grandma is really sharp and not at all gullible, so I have
8   to at least consider that what she tells me has really happened.
9   It seems the two of them had talked a long time ago about
10   whether there's any kind of life after death. Does the spirit live on?
11   Does that former person still keep track of his loved ones and know
12   what they're doing? My grandparents promised each other that
13   whichever one died first, that person would try to send some sort of
14   sign if he could, to show that he still existed. "Send money," Grandma
15   had joked. Grandpa said, "Pennies from heaven?" and Grandma said,
16   "No, make it nickels. Better yet, send dimes!" And they had laughed.
17   Grandma's first dime showed up in the Park-and-Fly lot near the
18   airport. She was going to visit her sister in Wisconsin, and she was
19   feeling really sad and uneasy about flying alone. She and Grandpa had
20   always traveled together; she missed him a lot. She pulled into the
21   parking spot and when she got out of the car, there was a dime on
22   the pavement. She picked it up, thinking whoever had parked there
23   last probably dropped the dime when he got out his car keys.
24   Then Grandma got to the terminal, and when she bent to take off
25   her shoes for the security check, there was a dime on the floor. She
26   put it in her pocket with the first dime, then made her way to the gate.
27   She was early, so there were lots of empty seats. She chose one at
28   random, sat down, and found a dime on the arm of the chair. That's
29   when she decided that Grandpa was trying to tell her he was

1   watching, and that he was glad she was taking a trip.

2   The coins have continued to show up, but never when Grandma
3   is just walking down the street, or in the mall. They always come at a
4   time when she's feeling especially lonely, when she's really wishing
5   Grandpa was still here.

6   She went to one of my brother's baseball games, and found a
7   dime in the dirt by the bleachers. After months of avoiding a favorite
8   restaurant where she and Grandpa used to go for breakfast, she
9   walked in one day, chose the table they always preferred, and found
10   a dime on her chair. She even found a dime in her own garage when
11   she got out the Christmas decorations.

12   Grandma keeps the coins on top of her dresser. She says she likes
13   to see them there when she gets dressed every morning. She says
14   they make it easier to face each day as a widow.

15   I asked her how it would be possible for Grandpa to make a real
16   coin materialize where she would find it. She said she didn't know.
17   She said there's no way to prove that Grandpa put them there, but
18   there are lots of things that scientists can't prove that are still real.

19   I was nervous about giving this monolog. I never spoke in front of
20   an audience before, and I was afraid you would laugh and make fun
21   of the whole idea of dimes as a gift from somebody who has died. But
22   as I walked out here, look what I found on the floor. *(Holds up a dime.)*
23   Thanks, Grandpa.

21. Mom Would Never Say This

1   My mother talks a lot. She watches the news and reads a
2   newspaper every day, so she can discuss current events. Since she's
3   active in the PTA, she knows what's going on at my school. She likes
4   to talk to her friends, and to her own mom, and to my dad. When she
5   talks to me, though, she mostly says stuff like, "Are you almost ready?
6   We have to leave in five minutes." Or, "Don't forget, it's your turn to
7   do the dishes."

8   There are some things I know my mom will never say to me, no
9   matter how much I wish she would. Here are ten of them:

10   One: "It's perfectly OK if you leave your dirty clothes on the floor,
11 instead of putting them in the hamper. I don't mind at all picking them
12 up for you before I do the laundry."

13   Two: "Yes, of course you can go to the midnight horror movie,
14 and I'll be happy to come and get you at the theatre at two AM. If
15 any of your friends need a ride home, I can take them, too."

16   Three: "Dad and I have decided to double your allowance. No
17 special reason except that you're such a great kid."

18   Four: "You don't have to do your homework tonight. Why don't
19 you just watch a movie or hang out with your friends?"

20   Five: "Aunt Shelly brought over a big pan of brownies. Is it OK
21 with you if we skip dinner and go straight to dessert? They smell
22 fabulous."

23   Six: "Instead of doing our shopping at the secondhand stores this
24 time, I'm going to drive you to the mall. Here's my credit card; get
25 whatever you want."

26   Seven: "You are certainly mature enough to see R-rated movies."

27   Eight: "Don't worry about cleaning up the bathroom when you're
28 finished. The tub needs a good scouring, and I was planning to mop
29 the floor anyway, so I'll take care of it."

1   Nine: "Would you like to borrow the New York Yankees sweatshirt
2 that Dad gave me for my birthday?"
3   Ten: "It's OK that you didn't start dinner as I asked you to. We'll
4 just order in a pizza."
5   Those remarks, of course, were wishful thinking. Here is what she
6 really said:
7   One: "Do you think I'm your maid? Either do your own laundry or
8 put your dirty clothes in the hamper."
9   Two: "Forget the midnight horror movie. I'm not driving around
10 in the middle of the night."
11   Three: "Your allowance is plenty. You just need to make better
12 choices about what you buy. We aren't made of money, you know."
13   Four: "No phone calls or movies until your homework's done."
14   Five: "Finish your veggies before you get a brownie."
15   Six: "We can't afford new clothes this year, but if you want to look
16 for bargains at Value Village, I'll take you there."
17   Seven: "No R-rated movies. Period. End of discussion."
18   Eight: "Excuse me, but you left a mess in the bathroom. You need
19 to scour the tub and mop the floor. Now."
20   Nine: "No, you can't borrow my sweatshirt. The last time you
21 borrowed something of mine, you spilled spaghetti sauce on it."
22   Ten: "You forgot to start dinner? Then you'd better fix sandwiches
23 for everyone, and you can have dinner duty again tomorrow."
24   Well, there you have it: what I wish she would say, and what she
25 really says. I have to admit, though, my mom does say one thing
26 exactly the way I want to hear it. She says, "I love you."

22. Changing Classes

1   My school has this pointless part of registration called "Choosing
2   an Elective." It sounded good the first time I saw it, but, believe me,
3   it is a total waste of time because the classes you sign up for are not
4   the classes you get.

5   I signed up for two electives this semester: Photography and
6   Beginning Piano. I was enthusiastic about both of them, but when I
7   received my schedule, two days before school started, I saw that I
8   wasn't in either of those classes. Instead of Photography second
9   period, I had Human Nutrition.

10   Now, I ask you: why do I need to study human nutrition? I am a
11   human who has been eating my whole life. I don't need to learn how
12   to eat. I also happen to have a mother who has been urging me to
13   consume more vegetables and to take a vitamin pill every morning
14   since I was old enough to understand what she's saying. I know all
15   about how Vitamin C wards off infection. I know my body needs
16   calcium to build strong bones. I know I need fiber to stay regular. I
17   drink orange juice and eat raw almonds.

18   I do not, repeat, *do not*, need to take a semester-long course in
19   human nutrition. What I need is somebody to show me how to use
20   my family's digital camera, and then how to hook it up to the
21   computer so I can send my photos to my friends. That is why I signed
22   up for Photography.

23   Human Nutrition wasn't my only problem. The class in Beginning
24   Piano, which I was supposed to have sixth period, didn't get enough
25   students, so the class got canceled. But instead of letting me select a
26   different elective to replace it, the school willy-nilly signed me up for
27   Introduction to Rock and Roll.

28   I happen to love classical music. The reason I want to take piano
29   lessons is so that I can eventually play Beethoven sonatas and Chopin

1 etudes. I do not want to play rock and roll. I don't listen to rock and
2 roll. I don't *like* rock and roll. And I certainly do not intend to spend
3 an entire semester studying rock and roll.

4   As soon as I received my seriously flawed schedule, I went to see
5 my advisor. "I have to change my two electives," I said. She frowned.
6 She said I would need to get the signatures of the instructors for
7 Human Nutrition and Introduction to Rock and Roll, showing that it
8 was OK with them for me to drop out of their classes. I pointed out
9 that I had never signed up for their classes, so why did I need
10 permission to leave? She told me this was the school rule.

11   Off I trudged to locate two instructors I'd never met and try to
12 explain why I didn't want to take their classes. The one who teaches
13 Human Nutrition was not there; she was on sick leave, which didn't
14 seem to say a lot for her nutrition. The substitute signed the release
15 for me.

16   The man who taught Introduction to Rock and Roll insisted I listen
17 to him play his guitar before I made up my mind. He strummed and
18 sang, and I tried not to grimace and cover my ears. When he finished,
19 he asked if I knew who had written the song he'd played. I shook my
20 head. "My favorite composer is Johann Sebastian Bach," I said. The
21 teacher put down his guitar, and signed my paper, giving permission
22 for me to transfer out of his class.

23   You may think that solved my problem, but oh, no. I still had to
24 find two electives that I could take. When I mentioned Photography,
25 I was told that all the Photography classes were already full. Through
26 no fault of my own, I was too late. I read the list of electives that still
27 had space. It was easy to see why they weren't full yet. It wasn't so
28 easy to decide which two to take. I finally chose Composting with
29 Worms for second period. No matter how gross it is, at least I'll have
30 a worthwhile skill if I ever decide to plant a garden, which I doubt I
31 will do.

32   For my other elective, I chose Conflict Negotiation. I figure what I
33 learn there will be useful next semester if I don't get the classes I want
34 and have to change my class schedule again.

23. How to Cure Insomnia

1   Judging from all the prescription drug commercials on TV, there
2   must be millions of people with insomnia. I used to be one of them.
3   Some nights, I did not get one bit of sleep. I lay in bed, sometimes
4   with my eyes open and sometimes with them closed, while my brain
5   raced from topic to topic. I wasn't worried about anything. I wasn't
6   scared. I wasn't unhappy. I also wasn't sleeping.
7   After awhile, it occurred to me that I might fall asleep more
8   readily if my cat, Furball, was not cutting off the circulation in my legs.
9   Whenever I lie on my back, Furball plops herself on top of me,
10   stretching herself out from my knees to my toes. It feels good at first
11   because she's warm, and she always purrs, but after awhile, not being
12   able to move my legs gets really uncomfortable. My feet grow numb
13   and my calves ache. That's when I try to shift position.
14   Notice I said, "try." Furball does not want to move. She digs her
15   claws into the blanket and hangs on. A six-point-magnitude
16   earthquake would not displace Furball. The only way to get her off is
17   to roll onto my side, which makes her slide down. Of course, all the
18   effort only wakes me up more.
19   Once I'm curled on my side, my dog, Harvey, notices that my
20   bent knees have now created a U-shaped place where he can snuggle
21   up tight. First, though, he has to scratch at the blanket and turn in
22   circles four times. Scratch, turn; scratch, turn. Harvey learned to do
23   this from his wolf ancestors, and he is diligent about following their
24   example before he flops down next to me. By the time he finally
25   settles himself, I might as well forget about sleep.
26   I know I could shut my pets out of my room at night, but the truth
27   is, even when they keep me awake, I enjoy their company. So I put
28   up with the cat on top of me and the dog scratching and circling
29   beside me, and I attempt to fall asleep.

1   One night I remembered an article I had read about self-hypnosis.
2   It told a sure-fire method for helping yourself fall asleep. I relaxed my
3   neck. I relaxed my arms. I imagined all my thoughts floating gently
4   out of the top of my head. But then, instead of continuing with the
5   relaxation process, I began wondering where my thoughts might go.
6   Would they enter my brother's brain? He was asleep in the next room
7   — I knew that for sure, because I could hear him snoring — so I
8   envisioned all of my thoughts shifting from my head to his. Did that
9   mean he would wake up tomorrow and suddenly like bagels, which
10   he always refuses to eat? Would he start saving his money instead of
11   trying to borrow from me?

12   I liked these possibilities, so I spent the next hour trying to
13   infiltrate my brother's brain by sending him my thoughts. I'm sorry to
14   say, it didn't work. He refused a bagel for breakfast in favor of some
15   disgusting cereal whose main ingredient is pink sugar. And while he
16   was eating, he asked me for a loan.

17   I was cranky from not getting any sleep, so I told him no.

18   I finally figured out the cure for insomnia by accident. One night,
19   after dumping Furball, petting Harvey, and staring at the dark curtains,
20   I got up, tiptoed out to the kitchen, and ate three chocolate chip
21   cookies. Then I crept back to bed, feeling guilty about not brushing my
22   teeth again, and promptly fell asleep. The next time I had insomnia, I
23   ate cookies again, and it worked that time, too. Now, any time I can't
24   sleep, I get up and eat some cookies. Sometimes it takes more than
25   three cookies, but, hey, you do what's necessary. It beats tossing and
26   turning all night long.

27   There's one slight problem, though. Now that I've cured
28   insomnia, does anyone know of a diet plan that works?

24. Ryan's Gun

1   Ryan brought a gun to school. He brought it three times, and lots
2   of kids knew about it because he showed it to them. He kept it in his
3   backpack, wrapped in a green towel. I saw it on the school bus
4   because I was sitting across the aisle from him. I watched him unwrap
5   the towel and show the gun to his buddy, Jason, who was sitting
6   beside him.

7   I didn't know what kind of gun it was; I don't know anything
8   about guns. But I did know that Ryan was not supposed to have one
9   in his backpack. There are signs on the edges of the school property
10   that show a black gun with a red circle and slash on top of it.
11   Underneath the picture it says "No Firearms Allowed on School
12   Property." Once a week, during the morning announcements, our
13   principal reminds us that there is a zero tolerance policy for guns and
14   drugs at school.

15   So I'm certain Ryan knew he wasn't supposed to have that gun in
16   his backpack. I thought about telling the bus driver, but I didn't do it
17   because I didn't want Ryan and Jason to hassle me for the rest of my
18   life. Even if Ryan got kicked out of school, Jason would be certain to
19   make my life miserable if I told.

20   Later, I learned that other kids knew about Ryan's gun, too.

21   Rachel told me she saw it during recess, when he showed it off
22   to a bunch of kids who had been playing basketball. The ball
23   accidentally bounced off the court and they all chased after it into the
24   empty field that adjoins the basketball court. Along with the ball, they
25   found Ryan sitting by himself with the gun in his lap. None of them
26   told a teacher. Rachel says she was too stunned at first to say anything,
27   and then the bell rang and she went back to class and got busy with
28   her history report.

29   When the police started asking questions, it turned out that lots

1 of kids had seen Ryan with that gun. Billy said he saw it in the boys'
2 bathroom. Ryan showed it to every boy who came in one day during
3 morning recess. When the police asked Billy why he didn't tell a
4 teacher, he said it was because Ryan said if Billy told, Ryan would
5 follow him home from school and shoot Billy's dog.

6   Aaron saw the gun in the bathroom, too, but he thought Ryan
7 was just goofing around. He said Ryan let him hold it and then made
8 a joke about how he could walk into the cafeteria for lunch and not
9 one person would suspect that there was a gun in his backpack. Aaron
10 said he never thought Ryan would actually use the gun. He thought
11 Ryan was just showing off in the bathroom, trying to get attention.

12   Other kids also admitted knowing about Ryan's gun. All of them
13 said pretty much the same thing: they didn't tell because they didn't
14 think Ryan would really use it, and besides, they didn't want to get
15 involved.

16   Now, of course, all of them wish they had told a teacher what they
17 saw. I wish I had told the bus driver, or my parents when I got home
18 that day. If just one of us had told, Kelsey would still be alive. Instead,
19 she happened to be in the library when Ryan stormed through the
20 door and started shooting.

21   Our librarian got shot in the leg, and her assistant was wounded
22 as they wrestled the gun away from Ryan. They got the gun, and they
23 sat on Ryan until the police came, but it was too late for Kelsey. She
24 died in the ambulance on her way to the hospital.

25   Ryan brought a gun to school. I knew it. Rachel knew it. Billy,
26 Aaron, and Jason knew it. Lots of kids knew about that gun, and all of
27 us wish with all our hearts that we had told. If we had, our friend,
28 Kelsey, would not have died.

25. What Do You Want to Be When You Grow Up?

1   Adults used to ask me, "What do you want to be when you grow
2   up?" I knew they meant did I want to be an artist or an athlete or a
3   firefighter, but I always felt as if the question implied I wasn't anything
4   now. As if kids are lesser beings who don't count yet. I wanted to be
5   noticed for who I was right then, not for what I wanted to be in twenty
6   years.

7   At first I answered honestly with whatever job currently appealed
8   to me, but the questioner often seemed taken aback, as if I wasn't
9   supposed to aspire to a career in worm farming. Once I was digging
10   happily in my sandbox when my aunt asked, and I said I wanted to
11   be a gravedigger. At the time, it sounded like a perfect career.

12   When my honest answers were not well received, I began saying
13   what I suspected the person who asked was hoping to hear. When my
14   doctor asked, I said, "I want to be a doctor, like you," and he beamed
15   and gave me an extra sticker. I told the woman in the bakery, "I want
16   to be a baker, like you." She gave me a cookie.

17   Those responses worked well until one day when my mom was
18   hosting her pinochle club. I was led out in my yellow jammies to say
19   goodnight to the ladies. One particularly large woman patted me on
20   the head and asked, "What do you want to be when you grow up?"
21   I replied, "Fat, like you."

22   After my mortified mother whisked me away, and told me no TV
23   for a week, I knew I needed to find a solid, dependable, honest
24   answer that would work every time and not get me in trouble. From
25   then on, whenever I was asked what I want to be when I grow up, I
26   said, "Old." That generally ended the conversation.

27   Now that I'm a teen, the question has changed to, "What do you
28   plan to do after you graduate?" The hoped-for answer is that I intend
29   to go to college. A full-ride scholarship to Harvard would be

1 impressive, but, unfortunately, I can't say that. I can't even say for sure
2 that I'll go to college. I have to make it through high school first, and
3 lots of days I'm not convinced that's going to happen.
4   If there is a diploma in my future, I don't know what I'll do next.
5 I'd love to take a year off and travel around the world, but I have no
6 way to finance that adventure. I wouldn't mind going to college if I
7 could study what interests me and not have to be quizzed on every
8 word I read. Right now I'm tired of tests and sick of studying.
9   Meanwhile, the next time I'm asked what I plan to do after I
10 graduate, I think I'll say, "I'm going to be either a brain surgeon or a
11 beach bum. I haven't decided yet."

26. The World's Worst Camping Trip

1   I know of families who go to Disney World or Switzerland for their
2 vacations. My family goes camping. Mom and Dad say camping
3 together creates lifelong family memories.

4   I'd like to go to Disney World or Switzerland, but I also love
5 camping because nobody cares if I get dirty, and we get to cook our
6 meals over a campfire. That's the best part — the campfire. Food
7 always tastes better when it's cooked outdoors, plus I'm always
8 starving from doing so much hiking and from throwing rocks in the
9 creek.

10   We have a favorite campground. It's never crowded and there's
11 this creek that's shallow enough to wade in on hot days, or to throw
12 rocks in, or to sail boats made of twigs and leaves.

13   One year, the camping trip was a disaster. Each person got to
14 choose the menu for one meal. It didn't take me long to decide. My
15 favorite camp meal is hot dogs roasted on a stick, followed by
16 s'mores. On the slight chance that someone here doesn't know what
17 s'mores are, I'll tell you. You toast a marshmallow over hot coals until
18 it's puffed up and tan colored. When it's just about to drop off the
19 stick, you put it on a square of graham cracker, mash it down with a
20 piece of chocolate bar, and put another graham cracker on top. Oh,
21 yum! I get hungry just thinking about making s'mores.

22   As usual, it took us longer to pack the car than we thought it
23 would and then we had to go back once because my little sister,
24 Mandy, had forgotten her blankie, and we all knew it would be easier
25 to go back and get it than to listen to her cry every night because she
26 couldn't go to sleep without the blankie to suck on. Mandy is almost
27 five, but she acts like an infant.

28   It was almost dark when we finally pulled into camp, but our
29 favorite campsite, which is way at the far end, closest to the creek,

1   was vacant. We nabbed it and hurried to get the tent erected while
2   we could still see. Mom said we would have my meal choice that first
3   night because it was so easy to fix. All we had to do was walk to the
4   ranger station to pay our camp fee and buy some firewood.
5   Dad and Mom carried flashlights, and I held Doozer's leash.
6   Mandy darted back and forth in the light beams, like a firefly.
7   I was thinking about those hot dogs; I like mine charred with
8   plenty of mustard, and sometimes I toast the bun for a minute, too.
9   And s'mores! Maybe I would make a double-decker, with two
10 marshmallows and two pieces of chocolate and a third graham
11 cracker.
12   I was so busy watching Doozer and planning my meal that I didn't
13 see the sign until I heard Mom say, "Oh, no." Then I looked up. The
14 flashlights illuminated a sign which said, "No Fires Allowed." Below it
15 in smaller letters, it said, "Due to the dry conditions this summer, no
16 fires of any kind are allowed in camp, not even in the designated fire
17 pits."
18   No fire? That meant no roasted hot dogs and no s'mores.
19   "Looks like we'll have to change our menu," Dad said.
20   "All the food we brought requires cooking," Mom said, "except
21 the trail mix that we have for snacks."
22   I asked Mandy what meal she had chosen, and she said,
23 "Pancakes and bacon."
24   My dad said he had picked spaghetti.
25   Mom had chosen what we call foil dinners, where you wrap foil
26 around a sliced potato, carrots, onions, and a hamburger patty, then
27 throw the foil packages in the hot coals.
28   We trudged back to our tent. Just as we got there, a humongous
29 RV pulled into the campsite next to us. We had purposely selected a
30 spot that was away from the other campers so we'd have quiet and
31 privacy. We plopped onto our camp stools and watched five little kids
32 and two big dogs spill out of the RV. The dogs raced over to sniff
33 Doozer, who seemed glad to see them. Dad wasn't, though. "Excuse
34 me," he called. "Dogs are supposed to be leashed in the
35 campground."

1   A man's voice hollered, "You kids tie up them dogs!"

2   Dad asked, "Anybody want a raw hot dog?" "No," I said, "but I'll
3   eat some graham crackers, marshmallows and chocolate bars." For
4   once, Mom didn't object to me eating dessert when I had not had any
5   dinner.

6   Usually we spend the evenings in camp sitting around the fire. I
7   love to poke at the fire with a stick or throw more wood on it.
8   Sometimes Dad tells stories. Mandy always falls asleep on Mom's lap
9   and has to get carried into the tent.

10   That night we sat outside listening to our neighbors yell at their
11   kids. Then we listened to their dogs barking because they didn't like
12   to be tied up.

13   Hunger pangs woke us up early the next morning. "We can't eat
14   raw pancakes," Mom said. "I vote we pull up stakes, find a good
15   restaurant, and head for home."

16   That's exactly what we did. It was a terrible camping trip, but
17   since then, every time we sit around a campfire making s'mores,
18   someone says, "Remember that time when fires weren't allowed?"
19   And then we all chime in, recalling cold s'mores and noisy neighbors.
20   Mom and Dad are right. Camping makes lifelong memories.

27. Mrs. Morse Is a Crazy Old Witch

1   Mrs. Morse is a crazy old witch. I had known it since I was five,
2   when I had to walk past her house on my way to kindergarten. All the
3   kids in my neighborhood knew it. The older ones told the younger
4   ones, whispering the news in their scariest voices: "Mrs. Morse is a
5   crazy old witch."

6   Sometimes the announcements got embellished. "Mrs. Morse
7   eats rats," they said, or "Mrs. Morse sets traps in her yard to catch
8   children who try to sneak close enough to peek in her windows. And
9   you know what she does to the ones she catches!"

10   I didn't know, but my imagination provided so many gruesome
11   possibilities that I nodded my head as if I did. I didn't want to hear
12   the words that would confirm my worst fears.

13   My older brother and his friends had never actually seen one of
14   the traps, nor had they witnessed Mrs. Morse dancing in the
15   moonlight with her pet boa constrictor, but their lack of direct
16   knowledge did not prevent them from telling me these tales as if they
17   were well-known truths.

18   I got chills down my neck when I thought of crazy old Mrs.
19   Morse, and I crossed the street a block before I came to her house
20   and stayed on the far side until I was well past it. No foot of mine
21   would be snared in a kid trap.

22   By the time I was in third grade, I had believed the Mrs. Morse
23   stories for so long that they were a fact. The earth is round, the sun
24   sets in the west, and Mrs. Morse dances with her boa constrictor. I
25   now passed my knowledge on to the preschool set, whose eyes grew
26   wide as they learned about the horror in their own neighborhood.

27   When I was in sixth grade, I got a job delivering newspapers for
28   a small weekly paper. I was to pick up my papers every Tuesday after
29   school and walk a fifteen-block area near my home, leaving a paper

1 on every doorstep. "Don't just toss it on the driveway or the lawn,"
2 my boss instructed. "Put it right next to the front door."

3   I was thrilled to be hired until I realized during my first day on the
4 job that one of my customers was crazy old Mrs. Morse. The last thing
5 in the world I wanted to do was walk up to her door. What if the boa
6 constrictor was lurking outside? What if Mrs. Morse thought I was a
7 burglar and shot me?

8   I delivered all of the papers except hers. I considered throwing it
9 away, but I was afraid Mrs. Morse would call the office to complain
10 that she didn't get her paper. I didn't want to get fired on my first day
11 of work.

12   I loitered across the street from Mrs. Morse's house for about ten
13 minutes, watching for a snake slithering in the grass. When I saw
14 nothing, I gathered my courage, dashed across the street, rushed to
15 Mrs. Morse's door, and dropped the newspaper on the doormat. Then
16 I fled, too terrified to look back.

17   The next Tuesday, I repeated the process except that time I only
18 paced across the street for five minutes. On week three, just as I set
19 the paper down, the door opened and I was face to face with Mrs.
20 Morse. Her white hair formed a halo around her wrinkled face. She
21 wore a faded pink sweatshirt and had a cane in one hand. She didn't
22 look at all witch-like, but I inched backward, just the same.

23   "Hello," she said. "I've been watching for you. I want to thank you
24 for putting my paper where I can reach it without going down the
25 steps." I nodded, but instead of saying "You're welcome," I blurted,
26 "Do you have a pet boa constrictor?"

27   Mrs. Morse looked astonished. "Good gracious!" she said.
28 "Whatever gave you such an idea? My only pet is Snookums, my cat."
29 As if he'd been waiting for his cue, a fluffy orange cat strolled forward
30 and rubbed against Mrs. Morse's ankles. "Good boy," she said. "Pretty
31 Snookums."

32   My heart quit pounding. I stopped backing away. As I looked at
33 the smiling woman and her cat, I realized that I had not been afraid of
34 Mrs. Morse, but of the unknown. I had believed the tales of traps and
35 snakes and craziness without one shred of evidence, solely because

1   other people told me they were true. I wondered what else I might

2   believe that's based not on fact, but on fear or ignorance.

3   I stepped forward and petted Snookums. Then I picked up the

4   newspaper and handed it to Mrs. Morse.

28. The Four-Part Plan for a New Me

1   A couple of months ago I read a self-improvement book and
2 decided to make some changes in myself. The book said to write
3 down four things about yourself that you'd like to change, and then
4 decide how you plan to change them.

5   You have to choose goals that are attainable. Don't say "I'm going
6 to be beautiful." Instead say, "I will shampoo my hair every day and
7 get a good haircut." Don't decide to be the most popular kid in
8 school. Instead, vow to be friendly to everyone and get involved in
9 extracurricular activities.

10   I started the new me process by making my list of all the things
11 about myself that I'd like to change. The hard part of that was keeping
12 the list to only four items. I also wrote one way to improve each
13 problem; those became my goals.

14   First on the list of what I needed to change was my butt. I'm not
15 going to turn around to demonstrate why that came first. You'll have
16 to take my word for it that I am seriously challenged in the beautiful
17 butt department. My plan for improvement is to ride my mom's
18 stationary bike for twenty minutes every day.

19   Second on the list was my grade in science. I hate science, and
20 my grades in that subject stink. I know they'd be better if I would
21 finish my assignments. They'd go up if I paid attention in class. I can't
22 even imagine what would happen if I did my homework. For my New
23 Me Plan, I decided to start paying attention in class. Maybe I'll
24 gradually work up to doing the assignments and the homework.

25   Third on the list was my chronic lack of money. I get an
26 allowance, but I usually blow it on CDs or chocolate. What I really
27 need is a part-time job, maybe on Saturdays or a couple of days a
28 week after school. Ignoring the fact that I have no qualifications for any
29 kind of job, I put as my goal: Find a job that pays. A lot.

1   Fourth on my list of what I don't like about myself was
2   procrastination. This entry got to the real nitty-gritty of what's wrong
3   with me. I've always put off anything that faintly resembled work. If it
4   takes effort, I can find a way to postpone it.
5   My goal for eliminating procrastination started with: Read another
6   book about self-improvement, but so far I haven't gotten around to
7   going to the library to find another book.
8   And that's why the Four-Part Plan for a New Me is still just that: a
9   plan. So far I don't have a job, I'm still failing science, and my butt is
10 exactly like it was when I started my list.
11   The trouble with self-improvement is that it doesn't work unless
12 you take action. You don't see results unless you actually *do*
13 something.
14   So I threw out that list and made a new list of all the things I like
15 about myself. It starts with this: I like to do monologs — but you
16 probably guessed that already.

29. Going to the Dentist

1   I went to the dentist yesterday, and it was not a happy
2 experience. As I walked in the door, I felt the way I think my dog feels
3 when I take her to the vet. I didn't shake and whine, as Wiggles
4 always does, but I felt like digging my toenails into the threshold and
5 refusing to cross it. The last time we took Wiggles in for her rabies
6 shot, we had to pick her up and carry her inside.

7   The dentist's receptionist greeted me with a big smile and said,
8 "Good morning. How are you today?"

9   Now, what sort of question is that? Did she really expect me to
10 say, "Oh, I'm just wonderful, thank you. I'm so excited to be here to
11 get my teeth cleaned. I love having the hygienist scrape tartar off my
12 teeth and poke her little needle down inside my gums. Of course, I
13 really hope I have a cavity so that I get to come back, and have the
14 drill, and the suction thing that takes the spit out of my mouth."

15   If I had been completely honest, I would have told the
16 receptionist that I was only there because my parents said if I didn't
17 go, I couldn't attend the basketball game tomorrow night.

18   I would also have said that on a score of one to ten, with one
19 being "I hate it," and ten being "I adore it," a visit to the dentist ranks
20 about minus three.

21   I didn't say that, of course. If I insulted her, the hygienist would
22 probably scrape harder and accidentally let the suction thing remove
23 my tongue. So I just mumbled, "I'm OK," and found a chair in the
24 waiting room.

25   I started to read an interesting magazine, but I was only half
26 through when my name got called, and in I went. I have to admit the
27 cleaning wasn't too bad. The dentist has new equipment that doesn't
28 seem quite so invasive. I only jumped twice.

29   When the hygienist finished polishing my teeth with some gritty

1   powder that tasted like steel wool, she said the doctor would be right
2   in to check me, but she didn't see any cavities. I brightened a lot at
3   that news. No cavities meant I wouldn't have to come back. I wouldn't
4   have to face the drill or the spit-remover. I was downright cheerful
5   when the dentist came in. He poked around in my mouth a little and
6   confirmed that I had no cavities, and then, just when I thought I was
7   home free, he dropped the bombshell.

8   "You're going to need braces," he announced. "I'll speak to your
9   parents to recommend an orthodontist."

10   I was struck dumb. Braces?! I don't want braces! Everyone I know
11   who has braces hates them.

12   Once again, I felt like Wiggles. If I had a tail, it would definitely
13   have been between my legs. I trudged after the dentist out to the
14   waiting room and got there in time to hear him tell my mom why my
15   teeth must be straightened. He gave her a couple of orthodontists'
16   names. She looked almost as unhappy as I felt. As we walked to the
17   parking lot, she muttered, "There goes our vacation."

18   I tried to tell her I don't mind crooked teeth. I said I'd much rather
19   see the Grand Canyon than get braces. I said if I have to get braces, I
20   will be so traumatized that I'll cry myself to sleep every night and flunk
21   all my classes.

22   I won't, of course. I'll go to the orthodontist, and put up with all
23   the discomfort and inconvenience because I won't have any choice. At
24   least I'll end up with straight teeth when it's all over. I called my
25   cousin who has braces, and it turned out his orthodontist is one of the
26   names Mom got. He said he actually likes the guy and that the whole
27   thing won't be as bad as I fear.

28   I'll probably always dislike going to the dentist, but I don't dread
29   it quite as much as I used to, because the worst that could happen
30   there has already happened.

30. The Comet Kid

1   I never have enough time. My mom says I have the same twenty-
2 four hours each day that everybody has, but I don't believe that's true.
3 I think student hours, for kids my age, go by faster than, say, baby
4 hours or old granny hours.

5   A baby can take naps all day and play with his toes and stare at
6 the dog the whole morning. Nobody tells the baby to hurry up and
7 finish his homework.

8   An old granny can rock in her chair and knit and listen to music
9 as much as she wants. If she plays solitaire after dinner, she isn't told
10 to get a move on.

11   Adult hours last longer than kid hours. How many times have you
12 heard an adult say, "I thought today would never end," or, "The
13 afternoon at work just dragged."

14   I've never heard a kid say, "That soccer game seemed to take
15 forever." Or, "I wish I could go home; I'm tired of hanging out at the
16 mall with my friends."

17   Yes, I'm absolutely certain the hours that adults have last longer
18 than mine do. Probably there are only forty minutes in each of my
19 hours, instead of sixty. Or else my sixty minutes are somehow
20 condensed, like *Reader's Digest* articles, so that they seem the same
21 as regular hours, but they really aren't.

22   I go straight from school to soccer practice, then home for dinner.
23 After dinner, it's homework time, and in between all of that, I'm
24 supposed to do family chores. My parents posted this chore chart in
25 the kitchen with names and assigned chores for each day. My chores
26 for today are to take out the garbage and mop the bathroom floor.
27 Lucky me. I can hardly wait to get started on such excitement. Maybe
28 NBC or FOX will send a crew to cover the action.

29   If the media wants a real story, they should investigate why kids

1   don't have as much time as adults have. I know one thing for sure: I
2   never have enough time to finish my homework.
3   In science we're studying comets. I saw a comet once, when I was
4   little. My grandpa woke me up while it was still dark and carried me
5   outside and pointed to the comet — a bright ball in the sky, with a
6   long tail streaming out behind it. He told me that the comet we were
7   looking at could only be seen every twenty years.
8   "The next time you see this comet," Grandpa said, "you'll be all
9   grown up and accomplishing wonderful things. Think of me when you
10 look at it."
11   Later that day, Grandpa read me a book about comets to be sure
12 I knew what I had seen. It said that comets are fiery balls of gas that
13 go hurtling through the universe, leaving long tails behind them.
14   The comet's tail is really pieces of the comet that are left behind.
15 As the comet flies through space, bits of itself break off, and drift away
16 like the showers of sparks that burst from fireworks on the Fourth of
17 July.
18   I feel like a comet, as if I'm hurtling through my life, unable to
19 stop, while portions of myself break off and fly away. Pieces of me are
20 used up at school; small sections stay on the soccer field; fragments
21 fall each time I rush to another activity. I lose whole chunks to chores
22 and homework. Just call me The Comet Kid.
23   Some comets become shooting stars. So many pieces fly off that
24 eventually there's nothing left. They simply burn out and disappear.
25 Other comets keep going for centuries, continuing to leave bright tails
26 in the universe.
27   Which kind of comet am I? What will be left of me by the time I
28 graduate? Will I be burned up, and ready to drop out of orbit? Or will
29 I keep flying ever faster, a shining force that leaves sparkling
30 accomplishments in its wake?
31   I suppose that's up to me. Probably it will depend on how wisely
32 I use my time. I'm going to do my science homework now. Maybe if
33 I study hard, I'll figure out how to make my twenty-four hours a day
34 be as long as everyone else's.

31. My Family Is So Boring

1   I have the most boring family in the universe. They need to get a
2   life — all of them.
3   My dad is pathetic. He has this awful engineering job that's so
4   technical nobody knows what he's talking about. When he comes
5   home from work, he reads work-related journals because he says he
6   has to "keep up with his field." He goes to engineer conventions, too.
7   He's president of some society whose members are all engineers. I
8   can't even imagine how dull their meetings are.
9   My mom is just as boring, but in a different way. She works at a
10 health club, so she's constantly talking about how we need to get
11 more exercise and eat nutritious meals and take vitamins. Given a
12 choice between a salad and a hot fudge sundae, my mom would
13 actually choose the salad. She tries to reform the whole world.
14 Specifically, she nags at me about what I eat and tries to get me to be
15 more active. I wish she would get some outside interest and leave me
16 alone.
17 Then there's my brother, Lenny, the baseball addict, who spends
18 all of his time either playing baseball, or reading about baseball, or
19 watching baseball on TV. In between those activities, he goes to a
20 place with batting cages to practice his hitting, or he runs laps at the
21 school track to improve his speed.
22 Last night my family sat down to dinner together, which doesn't
23 happen too often, and everyone talked about their lives. It was as if
24 we came from different planets. My mom discussed a client who has
25 lost fifteen pounds and now looks terrific. None of us knows this
26 client, so who cares? My dad told about a project he's designing —
27 a bridge over some river I never heard of. Lenny let us know who hit
28 a home run yesterday and which pitcher currently has the lowest
29 earned run average in the Major Leagues. He also told about the

1 twelve-mile bike ride his Boy Scout troop took last Saturday. I
2 practically fell asleep listening to him.

3   When Mom asked me what I had done after school that day, I
4 shrugged and didn't say anything. Actually, I had chatted with my
5 friends on the phone. We had all watched the same TV show the day
6 before and we talked about why we didn't like it. Since my boring
7 family never watches TV except for baseball games, there was no
8 point telling them about my conversation. I had also watched the
9 cartoon channel for awhile, and then I played a video game. I'd had a
10 great afternoon, but I knew my family wouldn't think so.

11   After dinner, Dad opened his laptop and said he needed to catch
12 up on correspondence for the engineer's convention. Mom got out
13 her knitting. She makes hats to donate to a homeless shelter. So far,
14 she's knitted forty-three hats. She says the people who get the hats
15 are grateful for their warmth, but how boring is that, to knit the same
16 thing forty-three times?

17   While Mom knitted and Dad wrote letters, Lenny practiced his
18 clarinet. He's been practicing a lot because he's going to be playing a
19 solo in the next school concert.

20   I yawned and clicked on the TV. There wasn't anything else to do
21 because my family is so boring. They really need to get a life.

32. Pet Peeves

1   What annoys you more than anything? That's the question my
2   language arts teacher assigned for a short essay. She said we were
3   supposed to choose a pet peeve and write about it.

4   That assignment was a big problem for me — not the writing, the
5   choosing. There are so many annoyances in my life every day that I
6   can't possibly narrow them down to only one.

7   For example: the people on cellphones who only call friends who
8   are seriously hard of hearing. That is why the callers feel they must
9   shout into their phones in order to be heard. While they carry on their
10   conversation in the loudest possible voice, the rest of us are unwilling
11   listeners.

12   These loudmouths do it standing in line in the grocery store; they
13   do it in shopping malls; they do it at football games and in school. It
14   drives me crazy! Yesterday on the bus, I heard all the details of what
15   some man I don't know had done last weekend, and believe me, he
16   had a boring weekend. He finally hung up, only to dial another
17   number and repeat the whole story a second time.

18   Cellphone users also annoy me when they fail to turn their phones
19   off at movies, concerts, and other public places where a ringing phone
20   is a serious distraction. Even when an announcement is made at the
21   start reminding everyone to turn off their cellphones, some people
22   don't do it.

23   When my cousin got married, someone's phone rang just as the
24   bride and groom were repeating their vows. And it wasn't a simple
25   ring; it was one of those cutesy songs that lasted about ten seconds.
26   Everyone in the church glared at the offender — but the damage was
27   done.

28   Another pet peeve is those little postcard-size ads that fall out of
29   magazines. It is nearly impossible to read a magazine without having

1 half a dozen pieces of paper drop into your lap. If I want to subscribe
2 to a magazine that I'm reading, it's easy to find information on how
3 to do so without being buried in it.

4   Even worse than the loose ads are the magazines that arrive
5 drenched in perfume. Some smell so strong that I can't read them;
6 they give me a headache. I've noticed it's only women's magazines
7 that do this. Either the publishers of men's magazines are more aware
8 of how annoying those scents are, or else they haven't yet figured out
9 how to make a magazine smell like after shave.

10   Pet peeve number four is store clerks who ignore me while they
11 chat with each other or on the phone. I'm the customer, right? They're
12 supposed to take my money and ring up my purchase, right? Instead,
13 they stand off to one side behind the counter and gossip. I once
14 waited ten minutes to buy a box of computer paper because the only
15 clerk in the store was getting a telephone quote on his car insurance.
16 I would have left except I had a report due and I was out of computer
17 paper.

18   When I complain about things like that, my dad always tells me
19 not to sweat the small stuff. He says life is full of petty annoyances,
20 but it isn't worth getting all upset over them. I know he's right — but,
21 still, I can't help fuming when I see someone toss litter out a car
22 window or walk a dog in the park without cleaning up after the pooch.

23   The only good thing about all these pet peeves is that I had so
24 many of them. I got an A on my Language Arts essay.

33. Dust Bowl Memories

1   The storms came quickly upon us — huge, dark, rolling clouds of
2 dirt. It was impossible to get away, even by going inside. I was ten
3 years old then, in 1934, and my family lived in Kansas. We farmed.
4 Or, we tried to farm — until the dust storms settled over everything
5 and turned our land worthless.

6   Black blizzards of dust so thick I couldn't see four feet in front me
7 whirled across our farm, seeping in through the walls of our house.
8 Mama tried to seal the windows with tape, but somehow the dust got
9 through. I slept with a wet rag pressed against my face, but I still had
10 to rinse the mud out of my mouth in the morning and swab my
11 nostrils clean.

12   Dust climbed into bed with me and sifted itself all over the
13 kitchen. Mama couldn't bake biscuits because dust had got in the flour
14 bin. When Papa milked our cow, he covered the milk pail, but, even
15 so, the milk was dirty before he could get it from the barn to the
16 house.

17   The storms came week after week for years. Dust piled up
18 everywhere like snowdrifts. It buried Papa's plow and covered the
19 road that ran past our farm into town. For the first time, I went to bed
20 hungry. We had no crops, and the shelves of our town's grocery store
21 were empty.

22   When Papa and Mama decided to move away, to seek a better
23 life elsewhere, we all cried. We couldn't sell the farm. Who would buy
24 land so parched it wouldn't even grow tumbleweeds? So we
25 abandoned it — we just walked away from that house I was born in,
26 where I'd learned to read and had celebrated every birthday, and we
27 left it to be buried in dust until it collapsed and was no more.

28   The hunger followed us, and so did the poverty. Papa had hoped
29 jobs would be more plentiful in Oklahoma, where we went, but the

1   dust storms were just as bad there. The Okies were leaving to start
2   anew in California, only to be greeted by highway signs informing
3   them that there were no jobs in California, and they were not
4   welcome there.

5   We tied everything we owned to our old Model T Ford, and when
6   the car broke down, there was no money to have it fixed. We left it
7   to rot, taking only what we could carry.

8   We walked with other dust bowl refugees and slept along the side
9   of the road at night, praying that the water in our canteens would last
10   until we found a source to refill them. One day we helped another
11   family dig a grave for a child who had died of typhoid fever in the
12   night. We had no shovels, so we dug in the dirt like dogs until we had
13   a deep enough hole to ensure wild animals wouldn't find that child
14   and make a meal of him.

15   When I think back to those times, I remember the abandoned
16   homes we walked past, remnants of someone else's lost dreams.

17   I remember sand in my eyes, gritty and scratchy. I remember
18   wondering if I would go the rest of my life without being able to take
19   a bath.

20   I remember the dust.

34. No Present for Sophie

1   Yesterday was my sister's tenth birthday. Her name is Sophie, but
2 I usually think of her as Stupid Sibling. Sophie is the most annoying
3 little sister ever born. She started following me around as soon as she
4 could walk, and she has never quit. Any time my friends come to my
5 house, Sophie tries to hang out with us, and if I tell her to get lost,
6 she sneaks around and tries to eavesdrop. When I complain to Mom,
7 Sophie whines. Sophie is an expert at whining.

8   Sophie gets away with murder because she's the youngest. She
9 is the baby of the family and can do no wrong. When Sophie does
10 things that I used to get grounded for, like forgetting to take out the
11 trash when it's her turn, my parents just smile and tell her to do better
12 next time.

13   Then there's the matter of her using my things without asking. If
14 I wanted someone else to come into my room and take my new
15 shampoo and use it, I would put a sign on the bottle that says, "Help
16 yourself." Believe me, there are no such signs in my room, but does
17 that stop Sophie? No way.

18   When I wanted to use my new gardenia shampoo, I looked on my
19 dresser where I had put it when I came home from shopping. It
20 wasn't there, of course. It was in the shower with soap scum all over
21 the outside of the bottle. Not only that, the bottle had tipped over and
22 all but two inches of the shampoo had run out. There was this gooey
23 pink puddle on the floor of the shower.

24   Then there's my set of colored pencils. These are really cool
25 pencils that have more than one color of lead in each of them, so
26 when you draw with them you get multi-colored lines. Sophie is
27 always trying to borrow them, and I know she sometimes uses them
28 when I'm not home because they'll need sharpening when I take
29 them out of the box, even though I always sharpen them before I put

1   them away.

2   Sophie makes me so mad that I decided this year I was not going
3   to give her a birthday present. Gifts are supposed to be expressions
4   of affection, given freely with no pressure. Well, ever since Sophie
5   stole my shampoo, I have felt no affection for her whatsoever. I didn't
6   have any to begin with, so now there's a minus on the affection scale
7   when it comes to my sister.

8   My family always celebrates birthdays the same way. The birthday
9   person gets to choose what we have for dinner, and then that person
10   eats off a special "Happy Birthday" plate. My grandparents always
11   come, and after dinner, the honoree opens presents and then we end
12   up with birthday cake. There are only family presents — kid parties
13   are held separately — so last night Sophie opened what my parents
14   and grandparents got for her. Other years, she would have had a gift
15   from me, as well. Not this time.

16   I thought this would be a fine way to punish Sophie for being such
17   a brat and wasting my new shampoo. I figured it was a perfect lesson
18   in Do Not Come In My Room and Use My Stuff. But it didn't turn out
19   quite like I thought. For one thing, Sophie was so excited to have it
20   be her birthday that she couldn't stop smiling. She didn't whine once.
21   She was thrilled with the books that Grandma and Grandpa had
22   bought for her. There were three of them, all by Sophie's favorite
23   author. She also loved the jacket and the new movie that Mom and
24   Dad had for her. She was so pleased by her gifts that she never noticed
25   there wasn't anything from me.

26   The trouble was, I noticed. As I watched Sophie open the books,
27   and the movie, and the new clothes, I felt strange. Always in the past
28   the best part of a family birthday was when the birthday person
29   opened *my* gift, the one I had chosen and wrapped. I would wait for
30   the honoree to select the gift I'd given. Then I'd lean closer and watch
31   carefully as it got unwrapped.

32   I never gave fancy, expensive presents. Once I gave Dad coupons
33   good for me to wash the car and bake him his favorite cookies. He
34   really liked that gift and turned in the cookie coupon the very next
35   day.

1   As I watched Sophie open her presents last night, I realized that
2   I wasn't having any fun. Everyone else was happy as they watched
3   Sophie open her gifts. Sophie glowed with excitement, thrilled to be
4   ten at last. She hugged Mom and Dad and Grandpa and Grandma and
5   thanked them for their gifts.

6   It was the worst birthday party I ever went to. I felt selfish and
7   mean. There was no satisfaction at all in not giving my sister a birthday
8   present. Instead I felt embarrassed, wondering what my parents and
9   grandparents thought of me.

10   When the last gift had been opened, Mom went out to the kitchen
11   to put candles on Sophie's cake. I dashed up to my room.

12   I got my box of colored pencils, found some gift wrap, and hastily
13   wrapped the package. Then I hurried back downstairs and said,
14   "There's one more present for Sophie to open before we have the
15   cake."

16   Sophie screamed with delight when she saw the box of colored
17   pencils. She hugged me and thanked me. For the first time since
18   Sophie's birthday party began, I smiled.

35. Names That Make Me Nervous

1   It seems to me that some things are not properly named. When
2   I go to the airport, for example, it makes me nervous that the building
3   where all the planes land and take off is called the terminal. *Terminal*
4   means the end. My dictionary defines terminal as "leading ultimately
5   to death."

6   People who have a terminal illness are not expected to live.
7   When I embark on a trip, I prefer to think that I'm going to reach my
8   destination in good health, so why should I have to begin and end the
9   flight in a building named terminal? Is this trip really my final
10 destination? I'm not afraid to fly, but I have to admit, I wish whoever
11 named the airport facilities had come up with something more
12 cheerful than *terminal*.

13 *Shot* is another word that ought to be changed. Most people
14 think of a shot as a bullet that flies out when the trigger on a gun is
15 pulled. Animals die after being shot by hunters. In war time, soldiers
16 get shot. Gang members with guns get shot by other gang members
17 with guns.

18 Getting shot is not painless or good; it hurts or even kills. There
19 is often a large quantity of blood involved. So why in the world would
20 the medical profession decide that vaccinations should be called
21 shots? A kid who needs to be protected from disease would be a lot
22 less fearful if he could be told he was getting a poke.

23 But no, the nurses and doctors all say they're going to give the
24 patient a shot. No wonder little kids holler and kick in protest. They're
25 afraid they might not make it out alive.

26 Then there's the administrative head of every school, who is
27 called the principal. This word, which means "chief" or "most
28 important," is accurate enough. The problem is that it's too similar to
29 the other word principle, which sounds the same but is spelled

1　differently. Every time I hear about a student being sent to the office
2　for discipline I think, "It isn't school I mind. It's the principal of the
3　thing."

4　　　The word that makes me most nervous is *diet*. Listen to the root
5　sound in that! *Die*-et. If that doesn't make you nervous about eating
6　too much salad and not enough apple crisp, there's something wrong
7　with your perception. A recent study shows that eighty-two percent
8　of teenagers are either on a diet or intend to start one soon. What's
9　wrong with these people? Don't they know that restricting calories
10　can be harmful to their health?

11　　　I say we should ignore all words that sound scary. Down with
12　diets and terminals and shots. Instead, fill your vocabulary with happy
13　words like *puppy* and *rainbows* and *fudge*.

36. Taking the SAT

1   I am so nervous! I took the SAT (Pronounced S-A-T) last week,
2 and I don't think I did well. It's hard to concentrate when you're
3 totally stressed out, and, believe me, I was stressed out that day. My
4 teachers had talked for months about the importance of the college
5 entrance exam. My parents had been talking about it for years. When
6 I was born, the timetable went something like this: Start solid food at
7 six months, potty train by age two, start preparing for the SAT at age
8 three.

9   According to the adults in my life, the day I took the SAT was the
10 most important day of my life because it would influence everything
11 that comes after it. Doing well on the SAT is crucial in deciding which
12 college I attend. Blow the SAT and I can forget any of the best
13 universities. They do not care to waste their time with students who
14 score low on any portion of the test. It isn't enough to ace the reading
15 comprehension if you are only average in math skills. Oh, no. You
16 have to be an all-around genius and score high in everything.

17   Two years ago, I was given a calendar that had an official SAT
18 question for every day of the year. Each morning, I was supposed to
19 read that day's test question and be sure I knew the correct answer.
20 I had SAT flashcards to study with, too.

21   Talk about pressure! For two weeks prior to the test, my parents
22 made me go to bed early each night, saw that I ate lots of vegetables
23 — especially spinach, which was supposed to increase my brain
24 power — and insisted that I re-read all the notes I had taken in the
25 course that was supposed to prepare me to take the test.

26   Yes, that's right. I actually took an online class that taught me how
27 to take the test. It was supposed to give me an edge — in fact, it was
28 "guaranteed to raise my score" — but all it really did was make me
29 even more nervous.

1 I'm used to studying for tests. I'm a good student, with above-
2 average grades, but I'm not used to studying how to take a test. I
3 learned to make sure I check either "True" or "False," even if I don't
4 know the answer to a true-or-false question, because if I check
5 something, anything, I have a fifty percent chance of guessing right.

6 The feeling that prevails is this: If I don't get a high score on the
7 SAT, and therefore end up attending a less prestigious college, my life
8 is pretty well botched up. I can forget about ever earning a good
9 salary or doing meaningful work. Romance is out of the question.
10 Score low on the SAT and you'll likely have to live with your parents
11 until you're forty because you won't be able to afford a place of your
12 own. Even your dog will hate you.

13 It's discouraging to think that my life is all downhill from here on.
14 Whatever happened to all those perky slogans? "Do your best; that's
15 all we ask." Or, "It isn't winning that matters; it's how you play the
16 game." For years I was told, "If at first you don't succeed, try, try
17 again." Only now I find out that there is no second chance. If I didn't
18 succeed on the SAT, it's all over. My hair will be greasy, my acne will
19 get worse, and I'll spend my days digging ditches.

20 There is one bright spot in all of this. If I didn't do well on the SAT,
21 it means everyone will have lower expectations. For the first time in
22 my life, maybe I can quit trying to meet somebody else's standards,
23 and just be myself. In the end, that might be better than four more
24 years of pressure to succeed.

37. Brussels Sprouts Are Not Comfort Food

1   Comfort food is a food you crave when you're troubled or
2 unhappy. Eating it makes you feel better. Comfort foods are different
3 from other foods. They're special, almost magical, and they differ
4 from person to person, which other foods don't do. What's a comfort
5 food for you might not be a comfort food for someone else.

6   My friend, Alex, for example, loves peanut butter and mashed
7 banana sandwiches. When Alex is feeling blue, nothing perks him up
8 faster than a peanut butter and mashed banana sandwich.

9   Personally, I like my peanut butter sandwiches made with grape
10 jelly. If I'm going to eat a banana, I prefer to peel it and take a bite,
11 not smash it all up with a fork until it resembles something you'd
12 spoon into the mouth of a six-month-old baby. Alex's comfort food,
13 which he likes better than anything, has no appeal for me.

14   Some foods are not comfort foods to anyone. Brussels sprouts are
15 not comfort food. Brussels sprouts are Brussels sprouts — they
16 furnish vitamins and fiber, but they don't provide sustenance for the
17 soul. I doubt there has been one single person in the whole history of
18 the world who would combat loneliness by eating a big bowl of
19 Brussels sprouts.

20   True comfort food lifts the mood of the person who eats it. It not
21 only provides calories for the body, it enriches the spirit. Comfort food
22 takes away your trials and energizes you when you're worn out.

23   My dad happens to love meat loaf. For him, meat loaf is a comfort
24 food. No matter what might be going on in his life, he feels happier
25 if he eats a slice of meat loaf. I think meat loaf is OK, but for me it is
26 not a comfort food. If my best friend picks a quarrel or I get a D-minus
27 on my math test, I don't rush home and look for some meat loaf.

28   Brownies, on the other hand, are comfort food. They not only
29 taste good, they soothe my stress. A thick, chewy brownie can go a

1　long way toward helping me forget that I didn't get a part in the
2　school play. A brownie, especially one with fudge frosting, can even
3　give me hope that it will be just as much fun to help backstage as it
4　would have been to be the star.

5　　My Aunt Ruth is always on a diet. Even when we eat in a
6　restaurant, she orders things like cottage cheese and sliced tomatoes.
7　She begins every meal with a salad, no dressing, and always refuses
8　dessert. But even Aunt Ruth has a comfort food.

9　　When her best friend got transferred and moved out of state, Aunt
10　Ruth ate buttered popcorn three times a day for a week. She said it
11　made her feel less lonely.

12　　That's what comfort food does. It helps you forget your troubles;
13　it gives you a reason to smile. I've read diet and nutrition articles that
14　warn against using food as a substitute for what's lacking in your life.
15　"Don't eat because you're bored," they say. "If you're unhappy,
16　chocolate won't fix the problem."

17　　I think the experts who write such articles know a lot about
18　dieting, but not enough about real life. When I have a problem,
19　chocolate will fix it every time.

20　　I think I'll go bake some brownies.

38. A Home for Katie
(A true story)

1   I volunteer at an animal shelter. My friends think I spend my time
2   there playing with kittens or petting puppies. The truth is, helping at
3   the shelter sometimes breaks my heart.

4   I was there when the social worker brought Katie in. Katie was a
5   black cocker spaniel, about eight years old, who had spent her whole
6   life with a homeless man. The man had mental problems. He
7   wandered the streets and slept under park benches or freeway
8   overpasses. Sometimes strangers gave him money for food;
9   sometimes he scavenged leftovers that other people threw away. He
10   always shared with Katie.

11   Katie did not get brushed or bathed. She never got flea
12   preventatives or vaccinations. Then her ears got infected.

13   She pawed at them and shook her head as if trying to get rid of
14   whatever was inside her ears. Her inner ears became red, itchy, and
15   swollen. So much scar tissue built up inside her ears that it was hard
16   for her to hear.

17   The homeless man realized that his dog was in pain, and he knew
18   she would not get better as long as she was with him. He loved Katie
19   too much to let her suffer, so he approached a social worker who
20   helped homeless people. He told her Katie was sick and said he did
21   not want her to be in pain. He asked the woman to take Katie to a
22   veterinarian and have her put down.

23   But instead of taking Katie to a veterinarian to be euthanized, the
24   social worker brought Katie to the animal shelter. She hoped some
25   kind person would be willing to adopt the dog and give her the care
26   she needed.

27   The shelter staff knew that Katie's chances of being adopted were
28   zero. In addition to the ear problem, her skin was infected from long-
29   term neglect. She was not spayed or housebroken, her fur was

1 clumped and matted, and she would have major veterinary expenses.
2 Why would someone coming to the shelter to get a pet choose a dog
3 like that when there were plenty of healthy dogs available?

4   My eyes filled with tears when Katie, in spite of her pain, wagged
5 her tail at me, and licked my hand.

6   The shelter manager called Pasado's Safe Haven, a rescue group
7 that takes animals deemed unadoptable. Pasado's vet examined Katie
8 and said she would need to have her inner ears removed. She would
9 be permanently deaf, but she would have no more pain. The surgery
10 would cost several thousand dollars.

11   Whenever a rescue group is faced with such a decision, they have
12 to consider how many animals could be helped with that much
13 money. Is it right to spend such a large amount on only one dog?
14 Katie could not go back to the homeless man. He loved her, but he
15 could not provide her with even basic care. Should all that money be
16 spent to save a dog that no one wanted?

17   Yet Katie had been a faithful companion, giving the homeless man
18 her devotion for eight years. The reward for such loyalty should not be
19 death; it should be a chance for a better life.

20   Pasado's decided to help Katie. Katie's matted black fur was
21 clipped off. After a bath, a soothing ointment was slathered on her
22 skin.

23   The best place to have the ear surgery done was the state-of-the-
24 art teaching hospital at Washington State University, in Pullman,
25 Washington — a seven-hour drive from Pasado's. Tina and Rick, who
26 volunteer at Pasado's, offered to drive Katie to the hospital in Pullman.
27 Several days later, after Katie's successful surgery, they returned to
28 Pullman to get her. Tina and Rick are foster parents for animals, and
29 they agreed to give Katie the care she needed until she recovered
30 enough to be put up for adoption.

31   For the first time in years, Katie's ears didn't hurt. Her skin didn't
32 itch. She had a warm bed and enough to eat.

33   Katie watched Tina and Rick's other dogs, and quickly learned to
34 go outside to go to the bathroom. Her skin infection healed, and her
35 fur grew back. She became a happy, playful dog, and it didn't matter

1   that she couldn't hear. She could see, smell, and wag her tail. She

2   became an expert at giving doggie kisses.

3   Tina, Rick, and their children fell in love with Katie. When she was

4   well enough to be adopted, they could not part with her, so Katie

5   became a permanent member of their family.

6   Now Katie is never cold. She eats plenty of good quality food,

7   sleeps in a soft, dry bed, and gets brushed every day. She has toys to

8   play with and people who love her.

9   At last, Katie has a home.

39. The World's Highest Cookie Stack

1   I've always thought it would be cool to have my name in the
2 *Guinness Book of World Records* . There are world records for all kinds
3 of amazing things, such as the world's tallest mohawk haircut and the
4 youngest kid to visit both the North Pole and the South Pole.

5   My friend, Eric, got in the *Guinness Book of World Records* by
6 playing his drum. The record he helped break was for the most
7 drummers playing the same song together in the same place for the
8 longest period of time. I went to hear Eric play when they set the
9 record. Talk about loud! It was fun, though, and it made me
10 determined to do something to get into the record book myself.

11   I discovered that the competition is fierce. Every single day, there
12 are thirty attempts at a new world record just in the United States! I
13 knew I would have to do something really unique.

14   My mother suggested I might qualify for Person With the World's
15 Messiest Room. My dad thought I could make the record book as the
16 Kid Who Procrastinates Longest When It's Time to Mow the Lawn. My
17 sister wanted me to try for a record as The Person Who Went the
18 Longest Without Talking, but I saw right through her plan.

19   I ignored all of my family's suggestions. Instead, I decided to try
20 for the World's Tallest Stack of Oreos. All I had to do was get enough
21 people to buy a bag of Oreo cookies and let me stack them up. They
22 could have their cookies back at the end, so they weren't out
23 anything.

24   I set the date and time for my effort. Then I got permission to
25 build my cookie stack in the school gym. I wanted to do the project
26 indoors, in case of rain, and the gym has the highest ceiling of any
27 room I could think of.

28   Soliciting people to provide cookies was easier than I expected it
29 to be. Most people thought it would be fun to be included, and many

1 asked if they could come to watch.

2 My bedroom quickly filled with bags of Oreos. Our garage held
3 boxes of cookies. Cookies were stacked on the piano and under the
4 table. It was worse than the years when my mom was a Girl Scout
5 leader and stored cookies at our house.

6 A reporter from the local newspaper called to say he was coming
7 and bringing a cameraman. That made me step up my efforts. I'd
8 never had my picture in the paper. I wanted to be sure my cookie
9 stack was newsworthy.

10 The World Record Cookie Stack Day was set for a Saturday. I
11 began hauling cookies to the gym as soon as school got out on Friday.
12 All of my friends helped and so did some kids I barely knew. We filled
13 our van, Mom drove to the school, we unloaded, and then did it
14 again. It took eight trips.

15 My two best friends, Mark and Sydney, were scheduled to
16 unwrap the packages so that all I had to do was stack up the cookies.
17 My plan was to make it a pyramid shape, with a wide base of cookies
18 that gradually tapered off as it got higher. I knew this would work best
19 because I had been practicing in my room. That's why sixty bags of
20 cookies were already opened, and the cookies were loose inside
21 pillow cases. All except the three I had eaten.

22 The Great Cookie Stack began at ten o'clock in the morning. It was
23 a stormy day with high wind and rain, but despite the weather, about
24 fifty people came to watch. By ten thirty, the stack was higher than I
25 could reach, so I put up the wooden ladder that I had brought. Mark
26 and Sydney handed me the cookies, and I continued to pile them on,
27 gradually making the circumference smaller. I was on the sixth rung of
28 the ladder, and the stack of Oreos was twenty feet high, when disaster
29 struck.

30 I stepped up to the very top of the ladder, feeling a bit precarious.
31 I had one bag of cookies in my hand and another tucked under my
32 arm. The newspaper photographer, who had been snapping shots
33 every five minutes or so, called out, "Look this way!" I looked. And
34 that's when the power went out.

35 There are no windows in the gym. It was complete, total

1 darkness. A couple of girls screamed. I tried to step down a rung, and
2 my foot slipped. I grabbed for the top of the ladder, dropping the bag
3 of Oreos. I lunged for it, lost my footing, and fell off the ladder,
4 straight into the stack of cookies. It crashed to the floor with me in the
5 middle of it.
6 　Oreos rained down on me. Oreos cushioned my fall. I ended up
7 flat on my back in a bed of Oreos, with more Oreos covering my lap.
8 I even had Oreos on my head. A bright flash of light briefly illuminated
9 the gym, followed by two more flashes. The photographer had caught
10 the whole sorry scene on film.
11 　I didn't make it into the world records book. I did get my picture
12 in the paper, though, sitting in a pile of Oreos with the headline:
13 "That's the way the cookie tumbles."

40. Gullible Gabe

1   My brother, Gabe, is the most gullible person in the universe. He
2   believes anything! If he hears a political ad on TV, he assumes that
3   everything the ad says about the candidate is true. If he gets an e-mail
4   that promises his dearest wish will come true in twenty-four hours
5   provided he forwards the e-mail to ten other people within ten
6   minutes, Gabe will type his friends' addresses as fast as he can and hit
7   "send." I don't know what he wishes for.

8   Gabe even believes those sob stories that come via spam about a
9   child who has cancer and can't afford the treatment, but if Gabe will
10   only send the message on to a zillion other people, some big
11   corporation will pay the cancer child a dollar for each one of those e-
12   mails.

13   I try to tell Gabe that these are hoaxes. They do nothing but clog
14   up cyberspace with unwanted messages. If some big corporation
15   wanted to pay the medical expenses of a child who has cancer, they
16   would just write out the check. What good does it do them for a
17   bunch of people to send e-mail all over the place?

18   Gabe does not believe me. When a letter warns that if he doesn't
19   follow directions, he'll be plagued with bad luck, then Gabe's afraid
20   to take a chance. Instead of deleting those letters, he does exactly
21   what they instruct him to do.

22   Gullible Gabe once told everyone he knew that a poem he wrote
23   had been accepted for publication in a book. It was a special
24   anthology for first-time poets. Gabe was thrilled! I asked if I could read
25   the poem, and this is what he gave me:

26   "'Dog Names'

27   I named my dog Blacky, but don't blame me.

28   I did it when I was only three.

29   If I were to name my dog today,

1   I'd call him Snickers or Milky Way.
2   Because my dog is oh, so sweet,
3   I'd name him for a favorite treat.
4   My dog would have a perfect name
5   If I could do it over again."
6   Now, I knew as soon as I read this garbage that no legitimate
7   publisher had chosen it for a poetry anthology. For one thing, *name*
8   and *again* don't rhyme, and the rhythm isn't right, either. We won't
9   even discuss the intellectual value of the subject matter.
10   I asked Gabe how his poem had been selected. It turned out he
11   had paid ten dollars to enter it in a poetry contest that he saw
12   advertised in a magazine. The ad said the winning poems would be
13   published, and, guess what, his was one of the winners.
14   I suspect every poem that was entered was one of the winners.
15   All of those ten dollar fees paid for printing the book and probably
16   gave a nice profit to whoever was running the so-called contest.
17   Two days after learning that his poem would be published, Gabe
18   was offered the opportunity to purchase copies of the book containing
19   his poem. For only twenty-four ninety-five plus six dollars shipping
20   and handling, he would own his personal copy of the book with his
21   poem in it. Naturally, Gabe ordered a copy. He wanted me to order a
22   copy, too, but I refused. I said I'd read his.
23   Gabe is very worried these days because he doesn't have any
24   money to wire to the widow of the King of Nowhere in order to help
25   her claim the three million dollars that she wants to split with him. She
26   keeps sending him urgent e-mails, but luckily he is unable to respond.
27   He can't wire the funds because he spent all his cash on extra copies
28   of his poetry book. He is saving them to give to his friends on their
29   birthdays.
30   Poor, gullible Gabe. At least his dog, Blacky, doesn't try to scam
31   him.

41. It's Not Worth Fighting About

1   I don't like fights. I don't even like arguments. I shy away from
2 confrontations and sometimes ignore insults rather than taking a
3 stand. I don't think this is necessarily a bad thing. In fact, I believe the
4 world would be a better place if fewer people were in such a hurry to
5 pick a fight.

6   Take road rage, for example. Yes, other drivers can behave
7 stupidly. They sometimes follow too close or cut in front of me or fail
8 to yield the right of way. But is that a reason to scream and curse or,
9 worst of all, pull out a gun? At most, the impolite driver might have
10 caused me to arrive five seconds later than I would have otherwise.
11 Is five seconds so critical that I have to blow my top like an active
12 volcano? I don't think so.

13   Sporting events are another place where people lose control,
14 along with their common sense. Some fans act as if the future health
15 of their children depends on their team winning a football game. They
16 swear at the officials, boo when a player makes a mistake, and
17 generally act obnoxious. Whatever happened to good
18 sportsmanship? Where is the fun in heckling the players and officials?
19 Could those fans throw a touchdown pass or make more accurate
20 calls? I doubt it.

21   Shopping can be dangerous, too, especially if you want to try for
22 one of the door-buster specials that are advertised during the holiday
23 season. I've seen people on TV who stood in line in the dark and cold
24 for hours in order to purchase a computer or the season's most
25 popular toy at a bargain price. There's nothing wrong with that —
26 what bothers me is when the doors open and there's a stampede,
27 with people rudely shoving past other people, trying to get to the
28 merchandise first. They seem to feel that getting a bargain computer
29 is so important that it's worth injuring someone else. I wish all those

1 shoppers would pretend that the other customers were their dearest
2 friends and relatives. Then maybe they wouldn't be so eager to
3 trample their way to the front.
4   I've thought a lot about this problem of rude behavior, and I've
5 decided that it's caused by lack of empathy. Empathy is when you
6 mentally put yourself in someone else's place and imagine how that
7 person feels. The absence of empathy causes war, poverty, hunger,
8 racism, homophobia, animal cruelty, child abuse, bullying, theft, and a
9 host of other serious problems.
10   Hit-and-run drivers flee the scene of an accident because they
11 have no empathy for the person they hit. Religious fanatics who kill
12 because of their faith have no empathy for their victims. School cliques
13 who snub a new student and teachers who humiliate a student in class
14 all lack empathy.
15   OK. I've convinced you of the problem. Now what do we do
16 about it? I think the solution lies inside each of us. If we would
17 regularly imagine how the people around us might be feeling, then try
18 to make them feel happier, there would be a lot less fighting.
19   Smile and say "Hi" to a new student at school. If it snows, shovel
20 your neighbor's walk when you shovel your own. Offer to share your
21 sandwich with someone who forgot his lunch. Hold the door open for
22 a person pushing a stroller. Stun your parents by cleaning up the
23 kitchen without being asked when you are home alone.
24   Will it make a difference? Can one person change the world? Yes.
25 Because what we do has a ripple effect, like a pebble tossed into a
26 lake. When someone is nice to me, it makes me want to be nice to
27 others. If you are kind to your neighbor, he'll likely be considerate of
28 someone else. That's the power of empathy. It keeps us from fighting
29 about things that are not worth fighting over.

42. Wagon Train West

1   The worst part was saying good-bye to my grandparents,
2 knowing I would probably never see them again. Until that moment,
3 my thoughts had been on what we were going to: the West,
4 California, the adventure of fresh sights. I had not considered that in
5 order to go to a new life, you have to leave the old one behind.

6   Two thousand miles in a covered wagon tests the strength and
7 determination of young men and women; my elderly grandparents
8 could not survive such a journey. When my grandma put her arms
9 around me and whispered her good-bye, I felt her tears drip on my
10 head, and I knew both of us were remembering the stories she had
11 told me and the ginger cookies we always baked together.

12   Now that we've traveled a few weeks, I know the other worst
13 part of this ordeal: there is no privacy. I loathe going to the bathroom
14 out in the open, and I always wait until I have no choice. There are no
15 trees or shrubs here on the plains to shield me from the view of the
16 others in the wagon train. The prairie grass, which stretches as far as
17 the eye can see, isn't nearly high enough to be of help. I avert my
18 eyes when others walk off the trail to relieve themselves. I pray they
19 give me the same courtesy, but I feel exposed, all the same.

20   I dislike bouncing along in the covered wagon or walking until my
21 legs ache when it's my turn to walk. My shoulders hurt, and I'd give
22 anything for a hot bath.

23   Most days we travel only fifteen miles — twenty on a really good
24 day. The oxen are slow because our load is heavy, even though we
25 brought only essentials with us: tents, tools, weapons, cooking
26 utensils, medicines, and food. Mama wept when she had to leave her
27 wedding china behind, but with the rough travel it would have broken
28 anyway. Papa promises to buy new china when we reach California.
29 When times are good again.

1   We left our chairs and our blanket chest alongside the trail
2   partway up a steep mountain, to lighten the load. All of us walked,
3   but even without our furniture we had to push the wagon to help the
4   oxen make it.
5   We were lucky. We left only furniture behind. One family's wagon
6   tipped over. All their food, so carefully stored and rationed, became
7   tainted and had to be thrown out.
8   The most cruel loss of all befell the Anderson family. They turned
9   back after their toddler fell from the wagon and was crushed under the
10 wheels. The men dug a grave and we all gathered for the burial, but
11 it was as if Mr. and Mrs. Anderson's will to continue had died along
12 with their son. When the sound of our hymn floated away and the
13 small body had been covered with dirt, the Andersons wished the rest
14 of us well and headed East, back toward Kansas.
15   That tragedy took a toll on the spirits of all of us. Mothers clutched
16 their babes more tightly; fathers shouted warnings to the older
17 children. Fear rode the wagon beside us.
18   Other dangers lurked along the way. Cholera struck frequently
19 and was usually fatal. A woman drowned when our group crossed a
20 river.
21   Is it worth all this sadness? Will our new life in the West be grand
22 enough to make up for such a toll? Papa thinks it will. He has a shining
23 vision of our future homestead with its sturdy log house and its acres
24 of fertile farm land. I think of my grandparents, and I hope Papa is
25 right.

43. Nursing Home Visit

1   As an experiment, my Scout troop decided that each of us would
2   do a random act of kindness and then report on how it made us feel.
3   For my act of kindness, I decided to visit Mrs. Ozborn. Mrs. Ozborn
4   used to live next door to us, but she's in a nursing home now. Her
5   husband died years ago — I never knew him — and her two sons live
6   in distant states. Mrs. Ozborn used to hire neighbor kids to help her
7   with chores. She hired me to pull weeds many times, and I always
8   liked working for her because she gave me a radio to listen to and she
9   had this old refrigerator in her garage that was stocked with soft
10   drinks and juice. She told me to help myself whenever I got thirsty.
11   As long as I put the empty can or bottle in the recycle container, I
12   could have as much as I wanted. I never had to ask.

13   Mrs. Ozborn paid well, too. We would agree on an hourly wage,
14   but when I finished, she always gave me a dollar or two extra. She
15   acted as if I was doing her a huge favor by coming to pull weeds
16   when actually I was always glad to get the work.

17   Whenever I had to sell stuff for school or Scouts, I could count on
18   Mrs. Ozborn to buy it. Over the years, I sold her gift wrap, cookie
19   dough, and candy bars. One year she bought all her holiday cards
20   from me. She always acted happy to see me, even when I had an
21   order form in my hand.

22   Mrs. Ozborn broke her hip last year, and when she got out of the
23   hospital, she went to the nursing home because she wasn't strong
24   enough to care for herself. Her house got sold, and a new family lives
25   there now.

26   My mom goes to see Mrs. Ozborn regularly, and she has been
27   nagging at me for months to go, too. I dragged my feet, not because
28   I didn't want to see Mrs. Ozborn, but because I didn't want to see her
29   there. I had been to the nursing home once before, when my Scout

1 troop went caroling. It is not a fun place. All of those elderly people
2 in wheelchairs or shuffling along with walkers — it's depressing.
3 Some are sick in their minds and thought the Scouts were their
4 relatives. One old woman tried to talk me into giving her a ride home.
5   What finally convinced me to go was when Mom asked if I
6 remembered the time Mrs. Ozborn had come to my school play. I was
7 in third grade and got cast as one of the seven dwarfs in a take-off
8 production of *Snow White*. I was thrilled! I loved the rehearsals and
9 felt so important about my part. I was terribly unhappy when I learned
10 my dad would be out of town on a business trip that week. He was
11 disappointed, too, but he said Mom would take pictures and tell him
12 all about it when he got home.
13   Then, on the day of the play, I got a note telling me to report to
14 the principal's office. When I arrived, I learned that my mom had fallen
15 and broken her ankle. She was at the hospital getting a cast put on,
16 and would not make it to the school in time for the play. I was
17 crushed. What fun is it to be in a play if nobody you know comes to
18 watch?
19   The cast members gathered right after lunch to put on our
20 costumes. When I was ready, I peeked through the curtains, hoping
21 Mom might have made it, after all. She had not — but there, right in
22 the front row, sat Mrs. Ozborn. She even had a camera! My sadness
23 flew away, and I could hardly wait to march on-stage singing, "Hi ho,
24 hi ho. It's off to school I go."
25   I glanced at Mrs. Ozborn as I entered. She beamed and gave a
26 little wave of her hand to show me that she recognized me in my
27 dwarf suit. When the play ended, Mrs. Ozborn clapped the loudest of
28 anyone and then she took a whole bunch of pictures of me.
29   Remembering the school play convinced me to visit Mrs. Ozborn.
30 The nursing home was just as I remembered, but Mrs. Ozborn was
31 much more frail than she had been. She was in bed when I got there;
32 her smile lit up her face when I walked in. She was so happy to see
33 me! I was glad to see her, too. We talked about the past, when she
34 lived next door. She exclaimed over how grown up I am, and asked
35 about my classes. I stayed for an hour, until the nurse told me she

1   thought Mrs. Ozborn was getting tired.

2   My Scout troop met the next Wednesday and I told them how I
3   had gone to visit Mrs. Ozborn. That night, my mom was reading the
4   paper when she gasped, and said, "Oh, no. Mrs. Ozborn has died."

5   I looked at the obituary photo of my friend. The smile was the
6   same one that used to greet me when I went to pull weeds or sell
7   candy. I was astonished to read that she had been an Associated Press
8   photographer — one of the first women to hold such a job. No
9   wonder her pictures of me as Sleepy turned out so well.

10   I am so glad I went to visit Mrs. Ozborn in the nursing home. I
11   can't imagine how awful I would feel now if I had not gone. I wish I
12   had gone sooner, and more often, but at least I did go. She knew I
13   remembered her; she knew I cared about her.

14   Mrs. Ozborn didn't know I was pushed into it by my Scout project
15   and my nagging mother. She thought I was there because I wanted to
16   see her again, and, in the end, that was true.

17   What began as an act of kindness toward my former neighbor
18   ended up being a kindness to myself.

44. Three Special Things

1　　There was bad flooding in my state last month. Many families
2　were evacuated from their homes, and some of the houses washed
3　away. I saw one family interviewed on TV right after their house had
4　floated down the river. They said they had been given ten minutes to
5　grab what they wanted to take with them. One of the kids was about
6　my age. After she carried her cat to safety, she said she chose three
7　special things. She didn't say what the special things were.

8　　I began to wonder what I would choose to take with me if I could
9　keep only a few items. It goes without saying that I would rescue my
10　dog and my guinea pig first. But what else would I take?

11　　After thinking it over for a long while, I decided what my three
12　special things would be.

13　　The first thing I'd take would be Roar Roar. Roar Roar is a stuffed
14　lion that my grandma bought for me when I was only two. I had seen
15　the lion in a department store when my mom and grandma were
16　shopping, and I was riding in my stroller. I climbed out, grabbed the
17　toy lion, and hugged him as hard as I could. When Mom pried him
18　away from me, I sobbed and held out my arms. She looked at the
19　price tag, shook her head, and told me she was sorry, but the lion was
20　too expensive.

21　　One of my earliest memories is of riding out of that store, feeling
22　bereft, aching to go back and get that lion. On my third birthday, my
23　grandma gave me the lion. When I opened her package, I was
24　flooded with joy. "Roar Roar!" I cried. "It's Roar Roar!"

25　　Since then, Roar Roar has sat on my bed every day, guarding my
26　room. I never actually played with him the way I did other stuffed
27　animals, but I loved him the most of any of my toys. Just looking at
28　Roar Roar brings back the feeling of astonishment that I had on that
29　long-ago birthday — the realization that impossible dreams

1   sometimes do come true.

2   The second thing I'd take would be the pictures that are on my
3   bulletin board. Every one of my class pictures is there, starting with
4   my kindergarten class. There are pictures of all my friends, of my pets,
5   of my cousins. There's one of our old house, where we lived when
6   Roar Roar came to stay. There are pictures from family vacations: my
7   dad holding up a big fish that he caught, me and my brother riding a
8   roller coaster, Mom and me wading in the ocean. The pictures remind
9   me of who I am and where I come from; I would not want to lose
10 them.

11 For my third special thing, I'd take the gingerbread boy cookie
12 cutter. I know that probably sounds like a silly thing to save, but that
13 cookie cutter symbolizes a whole lot about my life.

14 My dad made the cookie cutter out of tin. The gingerbread boys
15 it makes are about six inches tall. The first time I used it, I put the cut-
16 out cookies on the cookie sheet and then began experimenting. I bent
17 one arm upward, so that the cookie boy seemed to be waving. I bent
18 some of the legs so those cookies appeared to be running or jumping.

19 I gave some of the cookies raisin eyes, and some got chocolate
20 chip buttons. I pressed chopped walnuts around the head of one, and
21 flaked coconut on another, to make hair. I had a great time making
22 those gingerbread boys. After they were baked, I decorated each one
23 with frosting. Some got green frosting neckties; some got smiling red
24 lips. One got a yellow bow in her hair while others got melted
25 chocolate shoes. One had a white frosting shirt covered with
26 sprinkles.

27 All of this effort made a mess in the kitchen, and I had not yet
28 cleaned it up when my parents got home. I expected a lecture, but
29 instead, when my parents saw my gingerbread boys, they stared.
30 Then my dad said, "Those are wonderful! Each one is unique, just like
31 real people."

32 Mom said, "These are works of art. My gingerbread boys always
33 look pretty much the same, but yours are distinctive."

34 Then my parents hugged me. "You're original," they said, "just
35 like your cookies."

1   Since then, I have made gingerbread boys every December. I
2 always make each one different. And whenever I feel as if I don't fit
3 in at school, I remember that kids, like gingerbread boys, are better if
4 they aren't all alike.

45. How to Be Proactive in Math

1   My parents are always telling me to take charge of my life. "Be
2   proactive," they say. "Figure out what you want, then do what you
3   have to do to make it happen."

4   Well, that is easier said than done. Being proactive might work for
5   adults in the business world or when it comes to losing weight, but it
6   does not work for kids. It especially does not work at school. I know,
7   because I've tried.

8   I have a problem with geometry. My problem is, I don't get it.
9   Plain and simple: I do not understand geometry. But I do need to pass
10   the class in order to graduate. My parents said I should be proactive
11   about geometry. They said to figure out what I want and then make
12   it happen. It was easy to figure out what I want. I want to get a decent
13   grade in geometry so that I can get out of there and never think about
14   geometry again for the rest of my life. How to be proactive and make
15   that happen was a bit harder.

16   A logical person would probably say, "Fine. If you want to pass
17   geometry, you have to study." The trouble with that solution is that
18   in order to study geometry you have to understand what the textbook
19   says. I don't. I look at all those symbols and numbers, and it might as
20   well be written in some ancient language that nobody can translate.
21   How can I study what I don't understand?

22   Next step: stay after school and ask the geometry teacher for
23   help. I tried that, too. The conversation made me remember the first
24   time my family bought a computer. We went to a computer store to
25   look around, and the clerk started going on about megabytes and
26   fusers and system boards. Until that day, I had thought a hard drive
27   was the trip we made over a mountain pass to visit my aunt and
28   uncle. We needed to know how to turn the thing on, and instead we
29   got a college-level lecture delivered in techno-speak.

1   That's how I felt when I asked my geometry teacher to show me
2   how to do the problems. He tried to help, but he kept assuming I
3   knew what the terms meant. I did not, so his explanation was just as
4   confusing as the problems themselves.

5   Next I asked my cousin, Troy, if he would help. Troy is a whiz at
6   math, and he took geometry last year and aced it. Troy came over one
7   Saturday, but after spending an hour with me, he said some people
8   are just not meant to do geometry and suggested we shoot baskets
9   instead.

10   I finally went to the school counselor and asked if there was any
11   alternative to geometry that would meet my math requirements for
12   graduation. It turns out there was. She said I could take advanced
13   algebra instead. I promptly transferred from geometry to advanced
14   algebra. Even though I started late and had to make up what I had
15   missed, I got a B in the class, which is a whole lot better than I would
16   have had in geometry.

17   Maybe my parents are right. Signing up for advanced algebra
18   instead of geometry was a proactive solution. It didn't solve the
19   original problem, but it met my graduation requirement and, best of
20   all, it meant I wouldn't ever have to do geometry again.

46. The Squirrel War

1   My neighbor, Jenny, has an ongoing battle with squirrels.

2   Jenny likes squirrels, but she doesn't like having them climb up
3 her bird feeder and eat all the seed that she puts out for the birds.
4 Jenny enjoys watching the birds, and every morning she puts out
5 enough seed to feed them for an entire day.

6   Last year, squirrels began raiding the bird feeder. When the
7 squirrels came, the amount of seed that feeds the birds all day got
8 gobbled up in fifteen minutes.

9   Jenny tried a different feeder. Same problem. She tried putting
10 wire around the bottom of the feeder. No luck. She even tried taping
11 a piece of cone-shaped plastic on the post, but those wily squirrels
12 figured out how to get over it. No matter how she tried to thwart
13 them, they won every time. It's almost as if they enjoy the challenge
14 and can't wait to see what obstacle she comes up with next.

15   "Squirrels are cute," I told Jenny. "They have fuzzy tails and tiny
16 paws. Why don't you just feed the squirrels instead of the birds?"

17   "Because I like to watch blue jays and sparrows and flickers,"
18 Jenny said. "I prefer feathers to fur."

19   Finally, Jenny declared war. She purchased a humane trap, baited
20 it with peanuts, and put it near the bird feeder. Within an hour, she
21 had caught a squirrel. She loaded the trap in her van, drove to a
22 secluded forest area outside of town, and let the squirrel loose. "Bye-
23 bye, Squirrely," she said. "Have a good life."

24   When she got home all of the squirrel's relatives had gathered at
25 her bird feeder, looking for the one who was missing. Jenny reset the
26 trap, caught another squirrel, and drove it to the same location. She
27 figures if she turns all the squirrels loose at the same place, they'll find
28 each other and be happy in their new home.

29   Jenny was not pleased to return to her yard and find all the bird

1   seed eaten and two more squirrels waiting for a refill. She knew the
2   squirrels she had let loose could not possibly have hitched a ride
3   home. These were new squirrels. The question became, how many of
4   them are there? How many trips to the forest would Jenny have to
5   make in order to win the squirrel war?
6   Jenny borrowed a second trap so that she could transport two
7   squirrels at a time. The person she borrowed it from said she can use
8   it as long as she wants, but if she catches a skunk, she has to pay for
9   the trap and keep it. So far, Jenny has not caught a skunk, but she has
10 trapped and relocated forty-two squirrels, using up three tanks of gas
11 in the process.
12   I wouldn't have guessed there were that many squirrels within ten
13 miles of Jenny's house. She swears there is some sort of squirrel All
14 Points Bulletin calling for reinforcements at her address. Or maybe the
15 squirrels are trying to get themselves in the Squirrel Book of Records
16 for covering the most miles in the shortest period of time. The more
17 squirrels Jenny transports, the more new ones show up at her bird
18 feeder.
19   One thing is clear: Jenny either needs to buy more bird seed or
20 learn to love feeding the squirrels because in the war of the squirrels,
21 the squirrels are definitely winning.

47. Is Anybody Out There?

1   Late one night, as we drove home on a desolate stretch of road,
2 my dad and I saw a strange object in the sky. I knew it wasn't an
3 airplane, but what was it? It had a triangular shape, it appeared to be
4 made of metal, and it glowed with a bright white light.

5   Dad pulled off the side of the road and stopped the car while we
6 watched. The glowing object traveled low to the horizon, and fast. We
7 both thought it might have some kind of legs sticking out the bottom,
8 but we weren't positive of that. Dad took a picture with his cellphone,
9 and then we watched until the white light disappeared behind a hill.

10   "What was that?" I asked.

11   Dad told me it was a UFO — an Unidentified Flying Object.

12   When we got to the next town, Dad found the police station. We
13 went inside and told the officer at the front desk what we had seen.
14 The officer listened and made some notes but I could tell he didn't
15 believe us. "Maybe it was a meteorite," he said.

16   Dad showed him the picture he'd taken. Unfortunately, it was
17 fuzzy, and seeing a still photo of the object was not the same as
18 watching the thing hover in the air, lighting up the Earth below.

19   "It's probably space hardware," the officer said. "Debris from a
20 satellite that dropped out of orbit and fell to Earth. The light you saw
21 could be a reflection from the sun."

22   We left, but neither of us was convinced that what we had seen
23 was a meteorite or debris that had dropped from a satellite. It had not
24 been falling straight down; it was traveling horizontal to the tree line.

25   Over the next couple of days, as Dad and I told people what we
26 had seen, we were offered many explanations. One man said it was
27 a flock of geese. No way. The photo might be fuzzy, but the object
28 definitely does not have wings. And geese don't glow. Another
29 person suggested that it was merely an odd shaped cloud, and

1   someone else thought we had probably seen a weather balloon.

2   A few people believed us. One man even said he had seen a UFO
3   himself once but that he had quit telling anyone about it because
4   everyone thought he was mistaken.

5   I've done a lot of research about UFOs in the two years since I saw
6   one. I've tried to find out if it's possible that there is intelligent life
7   somewhere in outer space, life that could invent a spaceship and send
8   it to explore the Earth. So far the scientists have no proof of such life.

9   Still, any time I'm alone outside after dark, my eyes scan the
10   horizon, searching for a triangular piece of metal that glows. I have not
11   seen it again, but as I gaze at the sky, my heart silently calls, "Hello?
12   Is anyone out there?"

13   Perhaps one day someone will answer.

48. Ghost Dog

1   For several years, a ghost dog haunted my house. My older
2   brothers had both seen him, and they told me what he looked like.
3   He was mostly white with a few brown spots, and he looked a lot like
4   a wolf. He also had big, sharp fangs that stuck out on the sides of his
5   mouth, which dripped saliva. Sometimes I thought I saw him, but I
6   was never positive. I heard him, though. He howled in the night —
7   a low, mournful howl that put goose bumps on my arms.

8   Usually Ghost Dog howled when I was almost asleep. I'd have my
9   eyes closed, and I'd be hugging my tattered blue blanket that I always
10   slept with, and I'd just be drifting off when I would hear it:
11   "Oooowwuuuu ..." My eyes always flew open, and my heart raced.
12   My whole body stiffened, and I would lie there waiting to see if Ghost
13   Dog howled again. He always did, and on the second howl I would
14   leap out of bed and rush downstairs where my brothers were either
15   doing homework or watching TV.

16   "Did you hear that?" I would ask. "Did you hear the Ghost Dog?"

17   Sometimes they said they had not heard it. I couldn't believe it.
18   How could they not hear the howling that was so loud it woke me
19   up? Other times, they nodded solemnly and said, "Yep. That old
20   Ghost Dog is unhappy tonight. He must be hungry." They never
21   actually said the ghost dog ate children, but the way they emphasized
22   the word *hungry* I was sure that he did.

23   I kept a box of dog biscuits in my room. On the nights when
24   Ghost Dog howled, I piled some biscuits just outside my door. I
25   figured if he was hungry, I wanted him to eat before he came
26   anywhere near me. It worked, too, because the dog biscuits were
27   always gone when I got up the next morning.

28   Because my brothers were so much older than I was, I never had a
29   babysitter. Tim and Mike were in charge when my parents went out.

1   One morning, I was sleepy and cranky after being terrorized by
2 Ghost Dog two nights in a row. When my mother had a hard time
3 getting me up for school, she said, "What's wrong with you? Didn't
4 your brothers put you to bed on time?"

5   I told her they had put me to bed but I kept waking up because
6 Ghost Dog had howled, and I was scared of him.

7   "What ghost dog?" my mother asked. Her eyes had that squinty,
8 suspicious look that she gets when she thinks one of her kids is trying
9 to put something over on her.

10   "The Ghost Dog that lives in our house," I told her. "The one with
11 the fangs, who howls because he's hungry. I don't want him to eat
12 me."

13   Mom sighed and rolled her eyes. "Have you noticed," she asked,
14 "that this ghost dog only howls on nights when your father and I are
15 not at home?" That's when I realized that I had been duped by my big
16 brothers. All those nights when I had trembled in my bed, they were
17 downstairs, howling and laughing.

18   Mom said she would take care of the problem. Late that night, my
19 dad came into my room. When I opened my eyes he whispered,
20 "Shhhh. We're playing a trick on Tim and Mike." He sat on the bed
21 beside me. Then I heard the most awful howl. "Oooowwuuuu.
22 Oooowwuuuu. This is Ghost Dog! Oooowwuuuu."

23   I heard the door to Tim and Mike's room open and knew they
24 were looking out. The howling continued: "Oooowwuuuu. Those who
25 have impersonated me are hereby sentenced to kitchen duty for the
26 next month. Oooowwuuuu." Kitchen duty meant my brothers would
27 have to do the dishes, carry out the trash, and mop the floor every
28 day. They hated kitchen duty. I giggled.

29   The howling stopped. My brothers went back to bed. I quickly fell
30 asleep.

31   And Ghost Dog never came to my house again.

49. Thrift Store Bargains

1   My clothes come from thrift shops. Except for my underwear and
2   my shoes, everything I own was worn first by somebody else. My
3   mom loves a bargain. She began shopping at secondhand stores
4   when she was in college because she couldn't afford the cost of new
5   clothes at regular stores. She discovered dozens of really good
6   bargains on designer label fashions, and she's bought all of her clothes
7   secondhand ever since.

8   By the time I was born, Mom had a degree and a job and a
9   husband. Her financial situation had improved, but she still bought her
10   clothes, and most of Dad's, at secondhand stores. When I arrived, she
11   saw no point in paying full price for baby and toddler clothes when
12   there were so many used ones available that had barely been worn.
13   Little kids usually outgrow their clothes long before they wear them
14   out, so I got outfitted right from the start at Value Village and
15   Goodwill and the Salvation Army Thrift Shop.

16   As I grew older, I started to feel self-conscious about my used
17   clothing. I was afraid I'd go to school some day wearing a thrift shop
18   jacket and have some kid come up to me and say, "Hey! That jacket
19   used to be mine. I got it for my birthday, but I didn't like it, so I gave
20   it to Goodwill." I thought I would die of embarrassment if that
21   happened.

22   Nobody ever recognized anything I wore. Instead, lots of kids
23   said things like, "Cool outfit. Where did you get it?" and I would say,
24   "My mom got it for me," or, "Oh, this has been around a long time."

25   Then one day I overheard a kid in my class saying his new winter
26   coat cost one hundred twenty-five dollars, and I knew that my winter
27   coat, new to me and nearly identical to the one hundred twenty-five
28   dollar coat, had cost fifteen dollars. That's one hundred and ten dollars
29   less! You can do a lot of fun stuff with one hundred ten dollars. That's

1   when I decided I liked wearing thrift shop clothes.

2   I had shopped carefully for my coat, reading the labels and
3   looking at the construction to be sure it was durable. I tried on two
4   coats and chose the one that was most comfortable. It looks great on
5   me, and instead of being embarrassed by my secondhand purchase, I
6   felt superior to the kid with the expensive new coat.

7   So the next time somebody complimented me on my clothes and
8   asked me where I got the outfit, I said, "At a secondhand shop. That's
9   where I get all my clothes."

10   Well, let me tell you, this created a buzz. People crowded around
11   wanting to know where I shopped. Somebody asked if the clothes
12   were clean, and I said my family always washed everything before we
13   wore it so it was as sanitary as any other clothing. I told them how I
14   got nearly new jeans and sweaters for as little as two dollars. Everyone
15   thought it was cool that I saved so much money and still dressed
16   nicely. Many of the kids said they were going to try shopping at the
17   thrift stores.

18   I hope I didn't make a big mistake by being honest. If everyone in
19   my school starts shopping where I do, there may not be any bargains
20   left for me.

50. Why It Took Me Four Hours to Make My Bed

1   I spend way too much time doing chores. My parents believe that
2 kids need to be responsible for cleaning their own rooms and should
3 do a share of the housework for the entire family. This is totally unfair.
4 I have so many chores that I spend all my time working and have no
5 time left to play or daydream or just be a kid.

6   Let me give you an example. Last Saturday I had planned to go
7 to my friend Brian's house to jump on his new trampoline. I got up,
8 dressed, ate breakfast, and was heading out the door when my
9 mother stopped me. "Did you make your bed?" she asked.

10   There was no point saying yes because I knew she'd find out the
11 truth anyway, and then I'd not only be in trouble for not making my
12 bed, I'd be in worse trouble for lying about it. I said, "No, but I'll make
13 it when I get home. I told Brian I'd be there at ten o'clock, and if I
14 leave now I'll just make it."

15   Mom informed me that I had to make my bed before I left, and I
16 also needed to pick up all the clothes that were piled on my bedroom
17 floor. She said the trampoline wasn't going anywhere, and it wouldn't
18 matter if I was a few minutes late. I trudged back upstairs. My messy
19 room wasn't going anywhere, either. Why couldn't that be what
20 waited?

21   Making my bed has always seemed completely pointless to me.
22 Every day I straighten the covers and put the bedspread on, and then,
23 in only a few hours, I take the spread off again and crawl under the
24 covers and get everything all messed up. Who cares if my bed gets
25 made?

26   The answer, obviously, is that my mother cares. I yanked on the
27 top sheet, pulling it up. But when I did, I could see there was a big
28 lump underneath it. I raised the sheet, and looked under. My cat,
29 Muffin, stared back at me. She was purring and kneading her claws in

1 and out, clearly ecstatic at the hidden nest she had created.

2 Well, I couldn't pile the blankets and bedspread on top of Muffin.
3 She'd probably suffocate if I did. But I also didn't have the heart to kick
4 her out when she was so happy. So I grabbed the Spiderman comic
5 that was on top of my dresser, and started to read. I figured Muffin
6 would come out soon, and then I could finish making the bed.

7 It was an exciting Spiderman story, and I forgot all about Muffin
8 and my unmade bed. I forgot about Brian's trampoline, too. When I
9 finished the story, I lay on my stomach and fished around under my
10 bed, looking for the other two Spiderman comics that I knew I had.
11 When I found them, I read them, as well.

12 By then I was hungry, so I went out to the kitchen and fixed
13 myself a tuna sandwich. I carried it back to my room and the smell of
14 the tuna roused Muffin, who stretched and emerged from under my
15 sheet. That's when I remembered that I was supposed to be making
16 my bed. I quickly jerked the blankets up over the sheet, smoothing
17 them out before Muffin could change her mind.

18 When I ran my hand across one spot on the blanket, my fingers
19 came away all sticky. I tried again. Something had been spilled on my
20 blanket. I sniffed. It smelled like honey. I remembered eating peanut
21 butter and honey on crackers in bed the night before. I didn't
22 remember spilling the honey.

23 I took the blanket off, carried it to the bathroom, and stuffed it in
24 the clothes hamper. I had to push to make it fit, and on one push, my
25 fingers slid down the inside of the hamper and hit something metal. I
26 pulled the blanket back out and dug under the dirty towels. There was
27 my brother's skateboard! He had told me not to bother looking for the
28 skateboard in his room while he was gone for the weekend because
29 he had hidden it where I would never find it.

30 A sly grin crept across my face. I could practice on the skateboard,
31 return it to the hamper, and my brother would never know the
32 difference. It isn't often that the younger sibling gets to put something
33 over on the older brother, and I was not about to miss such an
34 opportunity.

35 I carried the skateboard out to the sidewalk and spent a long time

1   working on my moves. I quit only when my legs got so tired I was
2   afraid I'd have cramps all night. I reburied the skateboard and put my
3   blanket on top. Then I went to look for a clean blanket.

4   When I opened the linen closet, the first thing I saw was the box
5   of computer games that my parents dole out as rewards when I finish
6   my homework. Otherwise, I'm not allowed to play them. So this is
7   where they keep them! I chose one that I hadn't played for a long time
8   and spent half an hour playing. Then I put it back, took a blanket, and
9   went to finish making my bed. I tucked in the blanket, then quickly
10 pulled up the bedspread before Muffin decided to try out the new
11 blanket.

12   With my bed made, I was headed for the door when the phone
13 rang. It was Brian. "Where were you?" he asked. I told him I had
14 started for his house before ten o'clock but my mother had made me
15 come back to make my bed. "I just finished," I told him.

16   "It took you four hours to make your bed?" Brian asked.

17   I said I'd explain when I got there, but he said not to come
18 because he was leaving to go to a movie.

19   And that's how I missed out on the new trampoline, all because
20 my family makes me do too many chores.

Also by Peg Kehret

Books for Young People:

Acting Natural

Winning Monologs for Young Actors

Encore! More Winning Monologs
for Young Actors

Adult Books:

Wedding Vows

Photo: Larry Karp

About the Author

Peg Kehret enjoys a dual profession: playwright and novelist. Her funny, heartwarming plays have been produced in all fifty states and in Canada, while her books for young people have earned a wide readership and critical acclaim.

Among her many honors are the PEN Center West Award in Children's Literature, the Golden Kite Award from the Society of Children's Book Writers and Illustrators, Children's Choice Awards from twenty-nine states, the Forest Roberts Playwriting Award, and the Henry Bergh Award from the ASPCA. Many of her books have been selected by the American Library Association for its Recommended Books for Reluctant Readers list. Her work has been published in Denmark, Australia, Norway, Portugal, Canada, Sweden, Scotland, and India.

Peg is a widow who has two grown children and four grandchildren. She lives in Washington State where she is a volunteer for animal rescue groups. You can learn more about Peg at http://www.pegkehret.com.

Order Form

Meriwether Publishing Ltd.
PO Box 7710
Colorado Springs, CO 80933-7710
Phone: 800-937-5297 Fax: 719-594-9916
Website: www.meriwether.com

Please send me the following books:

_____ **Tell It Like It Is #BK-B295**　　　　**$15.95**
by Peg Kehret
Fifty monologs for talented teens

_____ **Winning Monologs for Young Actors**　　**$15.95**
#BK-B127
by Peg Kehret
Honest-to-life monologs for young actors

_____ **Encore! More Winning Monologs**　　　　**$15.95**
for Young Actors #BK-B144
by Peg Kehret
More honest-to-life monologs for young actors

_____ **Acting Natural #BK-B133**　　　　　　**$15.95**
by Peg Kehret
Honest-to-life monologs, dialogs and playlets for teens

_____ **Wedding Vows #BK-B151**　　　　　　**$11.95**
by Peg Kehret
How to express your love in your own words

_____ **100 Great Monologs #BK-B276**　　　　**$15.95**
by Rebecca Young
A collection of monologs, duologs and triologs for actors

_____ **112 Acting Games #BK-B277**　　　　　**$17.95**
by Gavin Levy
A comprehensive workbook of theatre games

These and other fine Meriwether Publishing books are available at your local bookstore or direct from the publisher. Prices subject to change without notice. Check our website or call for current prices.

Name: _____ e-mail: _____

Organization name: _____

Address: _____

City: _____ State: _____

Zip: _____ Phone: _____
　❑ **Check enclosed**
　❑ **Visa / MasterCard / Discover #** _____

Signature: _____　*Expiration
date:* _____ / _____
　　　(required for credit card orders)

Colorado residents: Please add 3% sales tax.
Shipping: Include $3.95 for the first book and 75¢ for each additional book ordered.

　❑ *Please send me a copy of your complete catalog of books and plays.*

Order Form

Meriwether Publishing Ltd.
PO Box 7710
Colorado Springs, CO 80933-7710
Phone: 800-937-5297 Fax: 719-594-9916
Website: www.meriwether.com

Please send me the following books:

_____	**Tell It Like It Is #BK-B295**	**$15.95**
	by Peg Kehret	
	Fifty monologs for talented teens	
_____	**Winning Monologs for Young Actors #BK-B127**	**$15.95**
	by Peg Kehret	
	Honest-to-life monologs for young actors	
_____	**Encore! More Winning Monologs for Young Actors #BK-B144**	**$15.95**
	by Peg Kehret	
	More honest-to-life monologs for young actors	
_____	**Acting Natural #BK-B133**	**$15.95**
	by Peg Kehret	
	Honest-to-life monologs, dialogs and playlets for teens	
_____	**Wedding Vows #BK-B151**	**$11.95**
	by Peg Kehret	
	How to express your love in your own words	
_____	**100 Great Monologs #BK-B276**	**$15.95**
	by Rebecca Young	
	A collection of monologs, duologs and triologs for actors	
_____	**112 Acting Games #BK-B277**	**$17.95**
	by Gavin Levy	
	A comprehensive workbook of theatre games	

These and other fine Meriwether Publishing books are available at your local bookstore or direct from the publisher. Prices subject to change without notice. Check our website or call for current prices.

Name: _____ e-mail: _____

Organization name: _____

Address: _____

City: _____ State: _____

Zip: _____ Phone: _____

❏ **Check enclosed**

❏ **Visa / MasterCard / Discover #** _____

Signature: _____ *Expiration date:* _____ / _____

(required for credit card orders)

Colorado residents: Please add 3% sales tax.
Shipping: Include $3.95 for the first book and 75¢ for each additional book ordered.

❏ *Please send me a copy of your complete catalog of books and plays.*

DATE DUE